META-LEADERSHIP

The New Skill Set for The Era of AI and Web3

ANDREA IORIO

First Hardcover Edition

ISBN: 979-8-9886684-04
Written by Andrea Iorio

Copy Editing by Ana Silvani, Marissa Blose, and Matthew Harms.

Cover Art & Graphic Design by Vitor Brandolff

Interior Formatting by Jahid Munshi

Manufactured in the United States of America

Let's publish together!
www.webookpublishing.com

CONTENTS

INTRODUCTION

According to American folklore, a steel driver by the name of John Henry tested the strength of man compared to machines in the 1800s. John Henry was a broad-backed, powerful man who prided himself on being the best in the world at what he did – blasting large rocks with a sledgehammer, which was a necessary step in creating railway tunnels. Working together with a shaker, who positioned a chisel-like drill on the mountain rock, John Henry would then hammer the chisel with all the strength he could muster. He did this all day long.

One day, a businessman came to the railroad construction company with the intention of selling an innovative tool – a steam-powered drilling machine. John Henry didn't think twice about challenging the machine to a competition. He simply refused to believe the salesperson's pitch that such a machine was more efficient than any human being. The rules of the competition were that whoever drilled the most during a full day of work would win. With confidence in his machine and certain victory would lead to a sale, the businessman accepted.

The following day, the challenge began. The machine worked fiercely as its piston went up and down the mountain endlessly, methodically digging holes. What John lacked in precision, he made up for in strength and vigor. With each blow of the sledgehammer, the weight of a lifetime of work was deposited on the drill head, driving into the mountain, as he was cheered on by his fellow workers. The competition went on for hours and hours, with the drilling machine leading far ahead of John until something miraculous happened. The machine broke down due to the wear and tear associated with the work. John continued hammering more holes until he was certain of victory. Then, at the foot of the mountain, with his hammer still in hand and celebrating his victory, John Henry's heart gave out from the stress of the work. He died only moments after achieving victory against the machine.

The truth is, this is only one of several versions of the legend of John Henry. Despite varying details, all versions carry a glorious yet tragic ending of a man who refused to accept being replaced by a machine. He fought for his belief that man would always be ahead of technology and forever irreplaceable.

Imagine what would have happened if John Henry had survived though. More than likely, the businessman would have returned two months later with a redesign of the machine inspired by John Henry's techniques. John would have challenged the machine again, and he might have even won. Then, the businessman would have done the same thing two months after that, and another two months after that, until the day the machine's innovations would finally prove to overcome John Henry's strength, leaving him with two options: continue to fight or accept defeat.

This folklore perfectly sums up the competitive relationship between humans and technology that has existed since the beginning of time. It has become an even more conflictual relationship today, in the midst of digital transformation, where new technologies evolve faster and faster due to the exponential nature of digital technology. Exponential laws established over the last few decades are backing our digital revolution, including Moore's Law, which states the speed and capability of computers can be expected to double every two years. Then, there is also Ray Kurzweil's Law of Accelerating Returns, which states the rate of growth of any exponentially growing technology is itself accelerating over time and will eventually reach a point where it will be happening so fast that calculating it will become impossible.

Gerd Leonhard, a highly regarded futurist, is known for saying that technology is exponential, but humans are not. He advises us not to try competing with the machines, but rather focus on doing the inherently human things – what machines cannot copy. The same goes for leaders. Rather than compete to the death like John Henry, we can learn what to outsource to technology and rethink what we need to focus our efforts on.

In the early 2000s, I was attending high school in Italy. The world had just "survived" the Millennium Bug, a computer flaw projected to cause problems when dealing with dates beyond December 31, 1999, and wreak havoc on computers and networks around the world. Thankfully, it did not.

Meta-Leadership

Three months later, in March of 2000, the world was introduced to the dot-com bubble when the Nasdaq Composite stock market index peaked, growing 400% since 1995, then falling 78% from its peak by October 2002. We were then in the midst of the first wave of online business growth on the Internet. Purely digital companies like Amazon and Google were only a few years old, and a disruptive platform like Facebook was about to be launched from a Harvard dorm room. This new era of digitization was the concern of many scholars who foresaw a full transformation from analog to digital and were then only left with one question: When would everything in the world, as we know it, go digital? Not *if*, but *when*.

Yet, as I entered my high school classroom one winter morning in 2000 in Savona, a city in northern Italy with a population of roughly 60,000, digitalization was not the concern of my teacher. At approximately 70 years old, she quietly smoked her cigarettes in the middle of class and tried to conceal her age with heavy makeup. That morning, we went back to the origins of almost all languages and dedicated ourselves to translating a text from Ancient Greek.

Among the small, scrambled letters of another language, in a time running slowly, the word *metanoia* unearthed itself. Metanoia, meaning a radical change in one's thinking, was an invitation for me to embrace the change of the world and understand the deeper meaning of human development, which is in a constant state of transformation.

4

Fast forward to 2011. After completing my Master's in International Relations at Johns Hopkins University in Washington D.C., I arrived in Brazil with two suitcases in hand, but without a home or a job. At that time, Brazil was predicted to be one of the newest world powers. I bet on that chip by moving to São Paulo, the most populous city in Brazil and the economic and financial capital of Latin America. During my time in Brazil, I was taken into industries I didn't anticipate. After responding to a job posting on LinkedIn, I was hired as a commercial manager at Groupon, one of the fastest startups to reach "unicorn" status after popularizing the collective buying model. This experience afforded me the opportunity to live in various cities in Brazil, such as Belo Horizonte, Curitiba, and Salvador.

Years later, I took over the launch of an American app in Brazil that created new terms in the informal dictionary, such as "swiping" and "matching." Yes, I am talking about Tinder. In 2014, I spent nights sticking Tinder stickers on the streets of Rio de Janeiro and São Paulo and distributing swag at university parties across the country to promote the app launched by the Match Group. It eventually became a viral phenomenon, reaching the number one position among the top-grossing apps in Brazil by 2017. At that moment, I realized digital technologies created opportunities for businesses to grow exponentially, and I knew I wanted to be at the forefront of digital transformation.

After heading the digital transformation of the Professional Products Department at L'Oréal Brazil, I decided to dedicate my career to speaking at events and to companies about topics such as digital transformation, tech trends, artificial intelligence (AI), Web3, and their impacts on businesses, customers, and leaders. After all, many businesses and their employees still see technology as a threat to their existence. It can be challenging to keep employees engaged, creative, and productive in a professional environment that is already increasingly dominated by machines, and AI is replacing many of our cognitive capabilities and our jobs. When I reflect back on the legend of John Henry and his fight against the machine, I realize our greatest weapon to evolve in an increasingly digital world is neither to fight technology nor to emulate it, but to develop a new skill set that makes us complementary to technology, not substitutable. This is especially important for business leaders.

Yet, as humans and as a society, we have not proven to be ready for most of the technological revolutions over time. Let's take social media as an example. In Kevin Systrom's last interview for *The New York Times* as CEO of Instagram, he made a comment about social networks, which is a great analogy for what is happening now with the new skill set required of leaders in the digital era. He said, "Social media is in a pre-Newtonian moment, where we all understand that it works, but not *how* it works," He added, "There are certain rules that govern it, and we have to make it our priority to understand the rules, or we cannot control it." The same holds true with leadership. One of the few statements we can make in an unpredictable world is that almost nothing will go as planned, and we still don't have clarity on what we will actually be experiencing. In the face of such unpredictability, there is only one thing that can and must be done – prepare ourselves by developing the necessary skills to adapt to this new way of leading and doing business.

If you ask any leader today about their biggest concerns when it comes to leading their business, one of the challenges mentioned often is developing the skills necessary to lead their companies into the future. In companies of all sectors and sizes, in the US and in the world, the best leaders already know companies cannot fully enjoy the benefits of new technologies without also having to develop a new skill set. After all, what is the point of having very sophisticated tools to collect data in real-time from our business when we still do not have the analytical skills to make informed decisions based on that data? We cannot roll out sales management software to sales teams who are not trained to use them and fear this software might steal their job in the future.

The key to growing your business in the era of digital transformation, AI, and Web3 is not only the technologies we use in them, but the new leadership skill set needed to better make use of this technology and respond to new customer trends dictated by these technologies. Inspired by the Greek word metanoia, this type of leadership is what I call meta-leadership, and the skill set of a meta-leader is unlike any other skill set we have yet to develop.

In the book *Fundamentals of Human Resources Management*, skills are defined as "an individual's level of performance on a specific task, or the ability to do a job well that can be broken down into technical elements and behavioral elements." Skills are contextual – they change as our understanding of work changes – and they can and should be developed. When it comes to meta-leadership, soft skills are more important than hard skills, since hard skills are easily replaceable by AI and machines. Soft skills, however, are more difficult to develop and therefore not (yet) replaceable. The difference between hard and soft skills can be broken down based on three main characteristics of soft skills.

1. Soft skills are broad-ranging. Unlike hard skills, which are narrow, specific, and focused on the resolution of a predetermined task or problem, soft skills can be applied in any life situation or circumstance, including in business. A hard skill, like speaking French, might not do you any good if you are traveling to Japan, but being respectful, friendly, and open-minded will serve you in France, Japan, or whatever country you may travel to.

2. Soft skills are difficult to transfer. Hard skills can be taught by transferring knowledge from one person to another. Though soft skills can be taught, it is a much more internal process, and there is room for ambiguity, which makes them more difficult to develop and transfer to another person. We can teach a young child basic math, but have you ever tried to teach a five-year-old empathy?

3. Soft skills are hard to measure. While we can evaluate the coding abilities of the software developer we want to hire during the interview process, we can't as easily measure and evaluate their critical thinking or decision-making skills.

Soft skills have only recently been recognized as having importance in the business environment. In an analog world, a leader had to be an expert on their product or service, not necessarily their customer, which made hard skills a priority. As we moved into a digital world, the customer became increasingly empowered as a result of technology, forcing the leader to know their customer even better than their product or service, which required more soft skills. Similarly, in an analog world where formal education and IQ were predictors of success in the workplace, soft skills have never been a priority. Yet, as we continue to move through this digital era, leaders will need to focus more than ever on developing their soft skills and present a new type of leadership – meta-leadership – to navigate the world of Web3, AI, and the metaverse.

Meta-Leadership

CHAPTER 1:

The Theory Behind Meta-Leadership

You are running a race through a neighborhood in your city, and your smartphone is in your pocket. Though it may not be in your hand, the applications are running in the background: counting your steps, recording your geolocation, and relaying your information and data to the app developer, which, in many cases, shares them with third parties. They know your performance on the run, what people are around you, and which establishments would like to send you advertising. While you are running, are you online or offline?

You go to bed after a hard day's work and lie down with your smartwatch on your wrist, which records the quality and timing of your sleep at all times. When you wake up in the morning, you have all the data recorded in an app on your phone. Were you online or offline while you were asleep?

You want to indulge in your favorite band's concert with body and soul fully present, so you don't even take your cell phone out of your pocket to take photos, post to social media, or participate in the wave of cell phone flashlights at the high point of the event. A stranger behind you posts a story on Instagram, and it registers your presence. Friends recognize you and soon know where you are. Were you online or offline during the concert?

The truth is, we are now online almost all the time. The physical and digital worlds are so intertwined that Israeli historian Yuval Harari, author of *Sapiens, HomoDeus,* and *21 Lessons for the 21st Century*, believes we are among the last generations of homo sapiens on Earth, as we are already close to programming our bodies and our brains through technology. Companies like Neuralink, co-founded by Elon Musk and a team of seven scientists and engineers, are already performing experiments with programmable brain-machine interfaces that can make humans restore vision and enable the movement of muscles in people who experience paralysis. Open AI's ChatGPT, a generative AI bot, can almost perfectly replicate human reasoning and language when writing text. Advances like these make Harari's belief not too far from reality.

None of this is to say the human race will stop procreating and cease to exist, but we will see a new form of evolution far more rapid and advanced than in prior generations. While our current generations have shed many traits that served our Neanderthal ancestors well, generations in the not-too-distant future will be born with evolutionary traits that allow them to thrive in a world full of constant body modification such as genetic engineering, chip implantation, and directly "wiring" ourselves to an assortment of Internet of Things (IoT) devices.

This new species will have many hard skills enhanced by technology. But what about our humanity? We can either lose it as we become more dependent on technology, or we can enhance it by outsourcing to technology what it does best and use the extra time and energy to focus on our human skills.

We are now in the midst of the Fourth Industrial Revolution, namely the digital revolution. The expression began to appear sparingly in academic articles in the late 1990s. It gave futurists pause and put executives at large companies on high alert. It occupied the thoughts of those who saw piles of paper in banks, public institutions, and large companies with decades worth of data. When it came to predicting the future, few imagined it would be a much deeper transformation than simply turning what was analog into digital. What, at the time, was a revolutionary process that simplified the lives of millions was only the tip of the iceberg, and most could not comprehend what more was to come. Yet, it was a path of no return.

Think about how businesses have changed due to current technologies by following the evolution of the Internet. Web 1.0 arrived with the birth of the Internet in 1989 and fundamentally digitized information, submitting knowledge to the power of algorithms (a phase that came to be dominated by Google). It became a place to consume content via desktop browser access and dedicated, on-premise servers. It felt like almost overnight, we no longer needed dictionaries, encyclopedias, or atlases. Libraries only stayed relevant because they offered free computer access for people to search the web instead of looking for books, taking them home, and coming back.

Then, Web 2.0 arrived with social networks and applications on smartphones, digitizing people and subjecting human behavior and relationships to the power of algorithms (the phase dominated by Facebook). This created space for users to not only consume content stored on the cloud but also create their own. This is where the majority of us exist today. Not only is the sharing of knowledge digital, but human relationships can now be formed and nurtured without ever meeting the other person in real life, and knowledge can literally be created online using tools like interactive learning platforms, podcasts, webinars, instructional videos, and so much more than the static blogs we had in Web 1.0.

Now, what is Web3? Although there is no consensus on the definition of Web3, for our purposes, we can call it a new generation of internet services built upon decentralized technologies, where the computing infrastructure has moved beyond cloud computing to the edge by processing data at the same place it is collected, and internet services are AI-driven.

Think of Web3 as the final phase in digitizing the rest of the world. In Web3, all objects and places will be machine-readable (understood by a computer) and subject to the power of algorithms. According to Gartner, there are three pillars of Web3:

1. The Semantic Web, which is a manner of organizing data on the Internet in a way that machines can understand it similarly to the way humans can.

2. Artificial intelligence (AI), which is the ability of machines to perform, learn, and design tasks normally performed by humans.

3. Natural language processing, which is the ability of computers to understand human language by extracting meaning from context.

Similarly to Web 2.0, we will still be able to consume and create content, but one unique aspect of Web3 is that we will also have the ability to own our content, though it will be nothing like today, where the chances of piracy and resale with no profit to the original creator are very likely. Think about how often blog posts or videos on social media are now shared countless times across platforms to generate profit for others, often to the point where no one even remembers where they originated. In Web3, you will be the full owner of your data thanks to blockchain and tokenization.

Gartner's second pillar, artificial intelligence (AI), is not a new concept, and it isn't exclusive to Web3. The Turing machine is the first model of AI, which was developed by Alan Turing to decode encrypted messages from Nazi Germany during WWII, though the Turing machine was originally called a "thinking machine." The term "artificial intelligence" first appeared in 1956 as the title of the summer workshop event hosted at Dartmouth called "Dartmouth Summer Research

Project on Artificial Intelligence." This workshop was organized by young scientist John McCarthy, who, for two months, debated ideas around the so-called "thinking machines". However, as a result of criticism, which affected the investments in AI, all discussions were practically frozen between the 1970s and 1990s around the world (with a small period of optimism in between). Today, however, is quite different. The development of a number of technologies, such as more agile and stable computer hardware, the growth of cloud computing, and the explosion in the volume of data that feeds machine learning algorithms, has placed AI as one of the main topics in business technology.

AI is so revolutionary that one of the world's leading experts in the field, Andrew Ng, said, "Artificial Intelligence is the new electricity." When we think about the transformative effect electricity has had on our society, we can see it has now become a commodity everyone now has access to. Just like electricity, AI will transform every aspect of our lives and will become available for everyone to access.

The opportunities associated with AI and Web3 are enormous, and if you don't get onboard now, you're likely to fall off the radar altogether. According to an analysis by Emergen Research, the global Web3 market size reached $3.2 billion USD in 2021 and is expected to register a compound annual growth rate (CAGR) of 43.7%, reaching $81.5 billion USD in 2030. Another report from Gartner predicts that by 2026, 25% of people will spend at least one hour per day in the metaverse for work, shopping, education, social, and/or entertainment purposes.

This can create huge opportunities for businesses to identify ways to serve their ideal customers through Web3 concepts and technologies while their competitors refuse to adapt. From creating immersive experiences in the metaverse through marketing campaigns to improving transparency across our supply chain through blockchain and even making perfect simulations of our equipment for customers to test out virtually new products, the opportunities are infinite in the world of Web3.

When it comes to AI, statistics show the market is enormous as well. According to Precedence Research, the global artificial intelligence (AI) market size was estimated at US $119.78 billion in 2022, and it is expected to hit US $1.59 trillion by 2030, with a registered CAGR of 38.1% from 2022 to 2030.

In other words, AI and Web3 are bringing such profound changes to businesses that the leadership styles that have sufficed over the past several decades will no longer be effective in moving us forward. Therefore, we need a new type of leadership – meta-leadership. Ironically, years after I crossed paths with the term *metanoia*, meaning a radical change in one's thinking, the Greek prefix *meta-* has become part of our modern language as a result of the metaverse, which is challenging us to radically rethink our beliefs and vision of the world. Yet, leaders are not necessarily prepared to lead their businesses through the era of Web3 because its profound impact leave many leaders still asking the universal questions:

- What makes a good leader?
- What are their key characteristics?
- How do I become a better leader?

Leaders have always played an important role in society, whether they serve as tribe leaders, political leaders, business leaders, or even leaders of a family. As human beings, we have a natural tendency to look for figures who can guide us, especially through difficult times, and who we can put our trust in so we feel less alone, less lost, and safer. Even though these questions are universal and timeless, the answers have changed a lot over time.

In Ancient Egypt, leadership came from the endorsement of the Gods and was considered sacred. In Ancient Rome, leaders were born either by blood or through family succession. However, none of these circumstances would guarantee good leadership skills. Through the 19th and 20th centuries, the prevailing theory of leadership was the Great Man Theory. Proposed by Thomas Carlyle, the Great Man Theory is an assertion that certain individuals are born with certain traits that allow them to be great leaders of the human race, implying these traits cannot be developed. Have you heard the phrase "Great leaders are born, not made"? It's the same idea.

Some of these "natural born" characteristics were command and control, extroversion, strength, charisma, and so on. However, these traits are not universal and are dependent on context. A leader who excels at command and control may be an excellent military drill sergeant but a horrible elementary school principal. As these leadership theories have proven wrong over time, the most recent theory of leadership is one based on competencies as well as both hard and soft skills. It is an adaptable and flexible approach to leadership, which develops new competencies and skills as the external contexts demand it. In this case, leadership skills are dependent on context, or the spirit of the time, which is called the *zeitgeist* in German. Therefore, I propose the world of Web3 calls for leadership styles to be updated in the face of such new and profound changes in the *zeitgeist*.

In today's exponential world, technology changes so quickly that it is more important for a leader to constantly update their knowledge about products, services, customers, the market, and their skills to complement these technological advancements, rather than just retain knowledge or rely on innate characteristics. The leadership style we've inherited from an analog world simply will not work in this third iteration of the Internet. This new era calls for meta-leaders. But before we can understand the skills meta-leaders need to be successful in Web3, we need to understand the five universal responsibilities of any leader:

1. Setting a vision
2. Making important decisions
3. Understanding the customer
4. Managing innovation

5. Managing people

These responsibilities are universal and have not changed over time. However, when we put these five responsibilities in the current context, or *zeitgeist*, of Web3, they have different implications and require a different set of skills.

1. Setting a vision: Because of the high unpredictability of future trends in all industries as a result of the exponential rate of change in the world of Web3 and AI, leaders must update and reshape their vision regularly to keep up. There is no time to delay, and every second you waste can have exponential consequences. It is key then to update such vision in face of constantly new information.

2. Making important decisions: Web3 will generate an infinite volume of data, with a range as deep as monitoring a consumer's pupil dilation, which means data will become a commodity. This makes it the leader's responsibility to choose the most important control metrics for their business to make better sense of the data at hand and to make better decisions than their competitors.

3. Understanding the customer: Traditionally, leaders would be mainly experts about the product or service they would produce or sell, but in Web3, this becomes much harder since the customer is more and more empowered thanks to technology. Therefore, leaders must understand even more about the customer. All this is extremely challenging since customers are very complex and distinct and update their expectations and behavior constantly.

4. Managing innovation: There is a very low cost of experimentation and a greater possibility for learning from mistakes as a result of real-time feedback in the world of Web3. This allows us to be more tolerant of errors, as they end up being cheaper and more informative, and they consequently help us to be more agile in the execution of our vision.

5. Managing people: Decentralization and autonomy become fundamental to people management in a world of "trustless" technologies. Faced with these new organizational structures as a result of Web3, leaders can outsource the control of their teams to "smart contracts" and focus on more autonomous and decentralized management of their teams.

Due to these profound implications in the five key responsibilities of leaders, we need a new style of leader who can develop a new range of skills to respond to the changes in this new digital era of Web3. This is where the meta-leader is born, for which I propose a leadership model based on the new skills below:

- Reperception, as a radar to navigate the uncertain future of Web3.
- Data sensemaking, to deal with the infinite volume of data.
- Cognitive flexibility, to learn and understand the infinite facets of our customers and consumers.
- Antifragility, to maximize experimentation and learning from mistakes.

- Autonomous management, for people management.

These pillars are designed to wash away any uncertainties you have about leading your business through Web3 and AI. The only thing constant in life is change, but we can only skate by for so long before we are left so far behind it is impossible to catch up. This has been proven countless times throughout history as companies have vanished or become shadows of their once-great legacy because leaders thought they were above adapting to the new way of doing business.

As technology changes, leadership must, too, because all other change within an organization starts with the leader. Technological revolutions have always caused some degree of disruption, but what we are currently experiencing will be far greater than ever before because of the high degree of exponentiality. The playing field is about to become much more level with the same tools and resources available to companies of all shapes and sizes. Good leaders look for areas of growth, and the opportunities created by AI and Web3 will be more abundant. Now is the time to start planning and assembling your teams with that vision in mind, while understanding and developing the necessary skill set to become the meta-leader your company needs.

CHAPTER 2:

Understanding AI and Web3

Imagine a bank vault filled with rows of unlabeled deposit boxes. Each deposit box has a glass facade, allowing everyone to see the contents of the deposit box but not access it. When a person opens a new deposit box, they receive a key unique to that box, but making a copy of the key does not duplicate the contents of the box. In the same way, even though you have the key, the box is technically not yours; you only have the ability to access what's inside of it. Fabricio Santos from Cointelegraph first proposed this analogy to describe the way the blockchain works.

Blockchain is truly the new data infrastructure in the world of Web3. Currently, information on the Internet is collected and controlled by a few companies, such as Google, Facebook, and Apple, which give rise to very profitable new business models related to data-based advertising and data sharing. Such a concentration of power creates oligopolies, which stifle innovation over the long term because reliance on a few winners who control most of the Internet's data means smaller

23

companies struggle to build competitive solutions that would give people more choices in regard to platforms they want to use. In this model, users also have little say in how their data is used.

With blockchain, we can move from this siloed model of the internet to one that's more transparent, where data is public, verifiable, and under the control of its users. With a blockchain-based model, innovative companies have the data they need to build their businesses, and people can control what data they want to share, receive fair compensation for sharing their data, and have more choice in what platforms they want to use. But blockchain alone does not comprise all of Web3. When we think about Web3 and its main pillars, blockchain is its decentralized data infrastructure, but we have to account for the three other pillars, which you can see in the image in the next page.

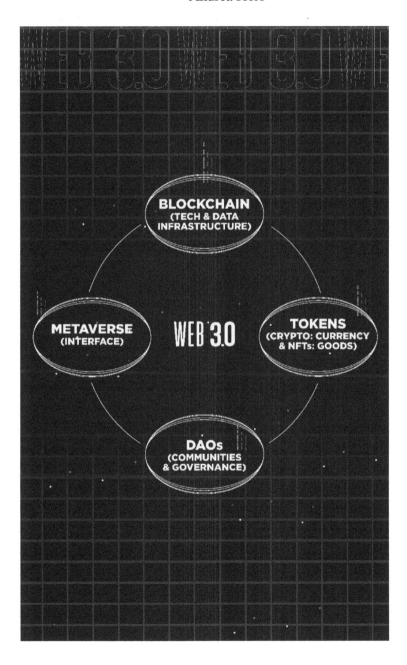

In addition to blockchain technology, the goods and currencies of Web3 are represented by tokens, which are digital representations of assets, access rights, or a combination of both, stored on the blockchain. They grant permission and/or ownership to a user, and they are a key part of how blockchain technology works, just like in the example of the glass boxes.

Governance in Web3 also changes. Traditional companies focus on maximizing shareholder value through a hierarchical organizational structure, where decision-making is centralized and in the hands of a few. In Web3, decentralized autonomous organizations (DAOs) become the new governance structure. Since DAOs are owned by their users, almost like a co-op, smart contracts on the blockchain expedite and democratize decision-making, which allows us to remove the agency problem by aligning interests across all stakeholders. DAOs basically make up for the new communities of Web3.

As the final pillar of Web3, there needs to be an interface. Although not exclusively, Web3 will pivot more towards an immersive, persistent, and decentralized interface, namely the metaverse. This buzzword is currently under scrutiny, but limiting the vision of the metaverse to Meta's ambitions of making it the ultimate place to socialize, work, and play is an unfair bias. It is much more than that because it represents the new interface of the Internet. In Web 1.0, the interface was mainframes; in Web 2.0, we had a mobile interface; and now, in Web3, we have the metaverse.

Because these concepts and technologies are crucial to understanding Web3, we are going to explain these concepts in depth to ensure you have the knowledge to back up your skills as a meta-leader. Although AI is not technically one of the pillars of Web3, we will also expand on AI and its impact on leadership skills in this section.

Blockchain, dApps, and Smart Contracts

A farmer from Tuscany in the 1400s was growing tomatoes to sell in the small village of Pienza. He set up a small kiosk in the city square and sold tomatoes directly to other villagers. The farmer was paid immediately, so he knew he had received payment for the tomatoes, and the villagers put the tomatoes directly into his basket, knowing they received the tomatoes in exchange for their money. There was little need for trust since the transaction was immediate, both in time and in place. However, if the variables of time and space change slightly, the need for trust grows. If a villager asks to delay the payment until the following week, the farmer must trust the villager will pay later. Similarly, if a villager pays right away but asks the farmer to deliver the tomatoes to his barn, the villager has to trust the farmer will make the delivery.

Faced with this problem and a lack of trust, the solution humans have traditionally relied upon is a trusted intermediary or middleman. If person A and person B don't trust one another, but they both trust person C, they can use their shared trust in the intermediary to facilitate a transaction. Examples of such intermediaries include banks, international credit card companies, escrow agents, distributors, retailers, and so on. But intermediaries are often inefficient, expensive, and retain too much power because they centralize information. To solve these problems in Web3, blockchain is introduced.

The easiest way to explain how blockchain works is through this quick experiment. Open Google Docs on your computer, and create a new document. Give it a title, jot down a phrase or two, then share it with friends, and ask them to do the same. By sharing the document, you have granted them access to it. Once they add their sentences, click on the "File" tab in the taskbar, scroll down to "Version History," and click on "View Version History." Here, you will see the entire history of versions and the changes made by each person at exactly what time they have been made, and you can fundamentally rebuild the history of the Google Doc in a transparent and collaborative way.

Could you do the same with a typewriter or in Microsoft Word on your PC? You could see the history of your edits if you have "Track Changes" enabled, but you wouldn't have the chance to build it collaboratively with others all at the same time.

This Google Docs analogy is the best way to understand blockchain in its simplest form, yet as the most important technological component of Web3. It may seem very complex, but the analogy shows us it's much easier to understand than we think. Blockchain is a decentralized and distributed digital ledger, or database, used to record transactions across the nodes of a computer network in a way that cannot be changed without the consensus of the network. It is basically a system of recording information from each individual computer (defined as a "node" in the network) in a way that makes it difficult or impossible to change, hack, or cheat, depending on your level of access.

A blockchain collects information together in groups, known as blocks. The blocks hold sets of information and are linked using cryptography, which is a technique of securing information and communications through the use of codes. Each block contains a cryptographic hash of the previous block (an equation used to verify the validity of data), a timestamp, and transaction data. Since blocks have certain storage capacities, when filled, they are closed and linked to the previously filled block, forming a chain of data that cannot be altered. All new information that follows the freshly added block is compiled into a newly formed block, which will then also be added to the chain once filled. It provides immediate, shared, and completely transparent information stored on an immutable ledger.

Think about how a database works today. They are centralized and rely on an intermediary to grant permission. For this to work effectively, you must trust these intermediaries. With the blockchain technology of Web3, it eliminates the need for both. Web3 doesn't require permission from an intermediary, which means central authorities don't get to decide who gets to access what services, nor does it require trust, meaning an intermediary isn't necessary for virtual transactions to occur between two or more parties. This leads to more data and user privacy. You might argue trust is still necessary for blockchain to work, and you're right – you need trust in the blockchain itself. But the trust lies in the protocol, not with those running it.

There are two main mechanisms to validate transactions on the blockchain and create new blocks on the blockchain: proof of work (PoW) and proof of stake (PoS). In a PoW blockchain, participants are called "miners," and they use their computational power to solve complex mathematical problems to validate transactions and create new blocks on the blockchain. Miners compete with each other to be the first to solve the problem, and the first miner to solve the problem is rewarded with newly minted tokens (in many cases, cryptocurrencies). This process is called "mining."

However, in a PoS blockchain, participants are called "validators," and they hold a certain amount of cryptocurrency as a stake, which then enables them to allocate their computational power to validate transactions and create new blocks on the blockchain. Validators are chosen to validate transactions based on the size of their stake. There is also a threshold for the minimum amount of stake to validate transactions. In other words, if you're below that threshold, you cannot validate transactions. If you're above that threshold, you can validate transactions no matter how high your stake is. Validators are incentivized to validate transactions honestly and accurately because, if they are found to be validating malicious transactions, their stake can be taken away. Similar to a PoW, validators who successfully validate transactions are rewarded with newly minted tokens. This process is called "staking."

PoS has key advantages over PoW because it consumes significantly less energy and doesn't require a large amount of computational power to solve complex mathematical problems. In addition, PoS is also considered to be more secure and more resistant to certain types of attacks, including 51% of attacks on a PoW network where an attacker gains control of a majority of the computational power. However, one disadvantage of PoS is the potential to lead to centralization, as those with the largest stake may have a greater influence on the network.

No matter which mechanism is used, blockchain will have all sorts of impacts on businesses. Let's take a pharmaceutical company as an example and consider all of its data from stakeholders, including patients, hospitals, doctors, pharmacies, and so on. There are several potential impacts, such as:

- Transparency: All of this data is tracked and shared transparently in real-time.
- Speed: You can access information in real-time rather than wait for intermediaries to supply it to you.
- Collaboration: All stakeholders can have access.

KPMG analyst Arun Ghosh said it best when he referred to the blockchain in the pharma industry as a "ledger of truth" for sharing complex information with regulators, pharmacy benefit managers, manufacturers, physicians, patients, academic researchers, and research and development (R&D) teams, and many others. This doesn't only apply to pharma, though; it's true for all industries.

Blockchain augments and even replaces the role of the trusted intermediary by creating trust directly between individuals through the use of computer software. This opens up an incredible new world for companies and consumers. While virtually every market has always had a need for an intermediary responsible for controlling transactions, from banks in the financial sector to notaries in real estate and retailers for consumer goods, blockchain is a way to eliminate the intermediary and decentralize everything. Instead of a bearded guy wielding a long-stemmed pen to record entries in a ledger, blockchain uses advanced cryptography and distributed programming (where multiple software components on multiple computers, or "nodes," run as a single system) to achieve similar results – a secure, transparent, and immutable record of truth, designed to be highly resistant to interruptions, manipulation, and unnecessary complexity.

Blockchain's ability to replace intermediaries through algorithms makes this technology important because it can reduce overhead costs when parties trade assets directly with each other or need to quickly prove ownership of information – a task that is currently nearly impossible without a central authority or impartial mediator. It also eliminates the big internet players like Google, Amazon, and Microsoft by decentralizing open and distributable data, so users can own their data and are free to share it without worrying about losing ownership or privacy.

The blockchain market has been growing steadily and is expected to grow faster and faster, with a MarketsandMarkets Research report forecasting a 68% CAGR throughout 2026. Although most of its use is happening in the financial sector, its use is growing in transportation, health, pharma, and fast-moving consumer goods (FMCG). Most of its use is related to a public blockchain, but there are other types of blockchains we will discuss in Chapter 8.

The best part about the blockchain is that accessing data and information and navigating Web3 won't be that different from what we experience now because the blockchain will be powering applications that can look exactly the same as the ones we access today, with the exception that they will be decentralized. This is why they are called dApps, or decentralized apps, which represent the "front end" of blockchain-based applications that allow users to interact with smart contracts deployed on the blockchain. Instead of employing the current HTTP protocol to communicate with the broader network, dApps connect to the blockchain in a decentralized manner, through computer network nodes, rather than routing through centralized servers.

There are a number of different blockchain platforms, but Ethereum is the blockchain platform that currently dominates dApp development because they implement a development interface that reduces the programming time and helps quickly launch projects through the Ethereum Virtual Machine. Beyond this, the Ethereum community has grown remarkably since the platform's launch, and Ethereum's blockchain continues to grow and add value as its network of global developers remains committed to maintaining the network and actively expanding user resources to make developing dApps easier. The more developers, the more valuable the blockchain becomes. The ability to adequately monetize dApp projects incentivizes others to partake in the Ethereum ecosystem. Other blockchain platforms include Hyperledger Fabric, R3 Corda, Ripple, and Quorum.

There are four main characteristics of d Apps:

- They are built on a blockchain.
- They are open-source.
- They have a reward system.
- Their functionality is determined by smart contracts.

The best way to understand how all of this works is through an analogy proposed by Nick Szabo, one of the pioneers of research in smart contracts and digital currencies. He proposes to think of dApps the way a vending machine works. It's the simplest transaction you can make – you decide what you want and insert the necessary amount of money into the machine. Once you click on the button or insert the code for the item you want, the machine automatically releases it. Smart contracts essentially work in the same way. These contracts automatically enforce themselves once certain conditions are met. This way, the only individuals concerned are those directly involved in the contract. There is no need for a lawyer, a notary, or any other intermediary.

Just like dApps are the "front end" of the blockchain, smart contracts are their "back end." They are programs stored on a blockchain that run when predetermined conditions are met. They usually work by following simple "if/when ____, then ___" statements written into code on a blockchain. A network of computers executes the actions when predetermined conditions have been met and verified, and once the transaction is completed, the blockchain is updated, meaning the transaction cannot be changed, and only parties who have been granted permission can see the results. Smart contracts are typically used to automate the execution of an agreement so all participants can be immediately certain of the outcome without time loss or any intermediary involvement. They can also automate a workflow, triggering the next action when conditions are met.

Let's say a traditional retailer sells products both online and in-store. One of the biggest challenges for the retailer is managing inventory, particularly when it comes to tracking the availability of products and ensuring they are in stock when customers want to buy them. This process could be greatly improved if the retailer uses a smart contract to automatically track inventory levels and trigger orders to restock products when inventory falls below a certain threshold. The smart contract could also be used to automate the purchasing process from suppliers. Rather than a supplier invoicing the retailer and the retailer sending their payment, a smart contract could automatically verify the supplier's shipment and delivery of the products, then automatically trigger payment to the supplier. This could ultimately reduce the risk of fraud or errors in the purchasing process. By using smart contracts to automate these processes, the retailer could save time and money while providing a more efficient and transparent service to their customers.

There are several advantages to having smart contracts on a blockchain over the current data infrastructure, and one is independence. You don't have to depend on intermediaries, and you don't need to trust them either. All you have to do is trust the system itself. Because smart contracts are decentralized, you don't have to worry about bias from any governmental body. Trust and security go hand in hand. If a thief wants to take your money, he could hack into your bank account. But because blockchain is decentralized, he would have to take over the majority of the network in order to gain access to your bank account or control anything.

Smart contracts aren't just secure and accurate; they're also fast. They eliminate the wait times for intermediaries like lawyers and notaries, and they are almost instant since the contract is enforced by the blockchain with a completely automated process. All of these advantages are beneficial to your business because they cut costs, increase efficiency, and prevent fraud by a third party.

Tokenization, Crypto, and NFTs

Some of the concerns many people have about Web3 are how to attribute ownership, store and exchange value, and determine what the currencies and goods are. The solution to all of those concerns is tokens, which represent the currency and goods of Web3. Tokens are assets that allow information and value to be transferred, stored, and verified in an efficient and secure manner. Tokens represent ownership over particular tangible and intangible assets. As a consequence, tokenization is then the process of converting any rights or assets into a digital token that can be used, owned, and transferred by the holder via a blockchain without the need for a third-party intermediary.

Tokens are basically the currency in the Web3 world, and they reward users for making the blockchain work. They can be used as rewards for people to contribute to the system through a mechanism called "token incentivization." This involves creating a system in which users are rewarded with tokens for contributing to the network in various ways, such as through mining or staking, which we discussed in the previous section. In both cases, users who contribute to the network by mining or staking are rewarded with tokens as an incentive. These tokens can then be used as a form of currency within the network or traded on cryptocurrency exchanges for other cryptocurrencies or traditional currencies. Tokens can also be incentivized as rewards through "bounties," which involve creating a bounty program in which users are rewarded with tokens for completing certain tasks or contributing to the development of the network in various ways, such as finding bugs, creating new features, or promoting the network.

Token incentivization can help to build a strong and active community around a Web3 network, as users are motivated to contribute to the network in order to earn rewards. This can help to increase the network's security, efficiency, and functionality, while also driving adoption and growth. However, tokens can be for much more than that. There are various types of tokens, but we can categorize them into three groups:

1. Security tokens: These serve as a digital representation of an underlying asset or utility. While not yet ubiquitous, security tokens are tokens that serve as direct, on-chain representations of real-world securities or tokens. In a case where a token represents ownership of an off-chain asset, such as real estate, equipment, payable invoices, or a business, similar to a share of stock, the security token's value is directly tied to the asset's valuation. The more valuable the asset, the more valuable the token.

2. Currency tokens: These are designed to be traded and spent. Some are based on physical currencies, like how Tether is tied to the US dollar; while others have a value determined by the distribution mechanism and the network. These tokens often function like traditional currencies, but in some cases, provide additional benefits. For example, with decentralized cryptocurrencies such as Bitcoin, it is possible for users to execute transactions without a traditional intermediary or central authority, such as a bank or payment gateway. Interestingly enough, not all transactional

tokens are currencies. Global supply chains and other industries can utilize transactional tokens to bring the transparency of the blockchain and the flexibility of smart contracts to their operations.

3. Utility tokens: These represent access to a given product or service, usually on a specific blockchain network, and are for practical uses, such as voting rights, powering a consensus mechanism, and so on. Usually, they are integrated into an existing protocol on the blockchain and used to access the services of that protocol. The relationship between a dApp platform and a utility token is synergistic, as the platform provides security for the utility token while the token provides the network activity necessary to strengthen the platform's economy.

Separate from the type of token, tokens can be divided into 2 big groups: fungible tokens and non-fungible tokens (NFTs). This categorization is related to the concept of "fungibility," which is the ability of a good or asset to be interchanged with other individual goods or assets of the same type. Fungible assets simplify the exchange and trade processes, as fungibility implies equal value between the assets. On a blockchain, fungible tokens are cryptocurrencies like Bitcoin (BTC). Fungible assets and tokens are divisible and not exclusive, similar to currencies such as the dollar. A $1 bill in New York has the same value as a $1 bill in Miami, just like 1 Bitcoin is worth 1 Bitcoin, no matter where it is issued.

Fungible assets are quite easy to understand, especially if you've ever been to Las Vegas and played at any of the casinos. There, you exchange a certain amount of dollars for an equal amount of tokens you can use to play. Fungible tokens are nothing new. They have been used in the form of gold and silver coins since the 17th century by merchants in North America and England as exchangeable collateral for material goods at times when state-printed coins were scarce.

On the other hand, non-fungible tokens (NFTs) are unique and indivisible. They are units of data that represent a unique digital asset stored and verified on the blockchain. They can be considered a kind of deed to a unique and non-replicable item. An airline ticket is not fungible because there cannot be another one of the same type due to its specific data. A house, boat, or car are non-fungible physical assets because they are unique. Based on their inherent characteristics, we can define fungible tokens as the currency of Web3 and NFTs as the goods.

NFTs are a record on a blockchain associated with a particular digital or physical asset that cannot be replicated. NFTs can also represent individuals' identities, property rights, and more. They are generally one of a kind, or at least one of a very limited few, and have unique identifying codes. Essentially, NFTs create digital scarcity, which stands in stark contrast to most digital creations that are almost always infinite in supply. Hypothetically, cutting off the supply should raise the value of a given asset, assuming it's in demand. If anyone can view individual images or even an entire collage of images online for free, why would anyone be willing to spend millions on something they could easily screenshot or download? Because an NFT allows the buyer to own the original item. Not only that, it contains built-in authentication, which serves as proof of ownership.

NFTs are not only digital pieces of art or just speculative items. Consider the possibility for healthcare patients to transform their medical data into NFTs and solve a big problem – over \$1.2 billion worth of clinical documents are produced in the US every year, yet 80% of that data remains unstructured and vulnerable to misuse and theft. Patients don't know where their medical data finally ends up after it's been collected. In a world of AI, big data is becoming increasingly important to drug research as sensitive medical information, like hospital records or genetic markups, has become an extremely valuable commodity. Many times, such data is bought, exchanged, or sold without the knowledge or consent of the patient. NFTs in healthcare can prove beneficial by allowing patients to control and monetize their data. Patients would be able to track their medical data, see where it has ended up, and hold those who have used it without their consent accountable. They would also get royalties every time they allow a company to use their data.

Here are some of the advantages of tokenizing an asset:

- It introduces more liquidity to the asset, which means it is easier to exchange and available to much larger audiences. The more liquid an asset is, the more easily exchangeable it is.

- It lowers transaction costs, bypassing market intermediaries and other middlemen, further reducing cost and processing time.

- It improves transparency since users can easily trace the asset origin and transaction history in a way that is cryptographically verifiable.

- It maximizes security since it is based on blockchain technology that is extremely secure and less vulnerable to attacks and fraud.

- It allows for interoperability, which is a feature of Web3 whereby a product or system can work seamlessly across platforms with other products and services. This reduces the friction in transactions that might exist today due to different standards in different geographies.

As an exercise, think about how tokenization can help a real estate company. To start off, liquidity is a clear advantage. Tokenization can solve the lack of liquidity and high transaction costs in real estate. Since the advent of Ethereum and smart contracts, many have dreamed of the benefits of tokenized real estate, and now it is happening. One of the biggest benefits of real estate tokenization is the ability to reduce investment amounts (from, say, $50,000 to $10) due to the technological automation of issuance and post-issuance processes. This lower requirement dramatically increases the universe of investors and, subsequently, the supply of capital and liquidity to investors. In fact, only 7% of all commercial real estate is available to investors, yet over 80% of individuals seek to have some type of investment in real estate as evident in the surge of capital flowing into crowdfunding sites. Tokenization will prove to be a solution to all this.

Decentralized Autonomous Organizations (DAOs)

If you are familiar with soccer, you likely know of the Barcelona soccer team. They have been one of the most dominant teams in the recent history of the game, with stars such as Lionel Messi and Neymar. One unique thing about their team is, unlike every other team in the league, they aren't owned outright by a single individual. Instead, they are owned by their fans. Barcelona is a members-owned club with over 144,000 members, many of whom are fans, and they make decisions regarding the future direction of the club. Their club motto, "Más Que Un Club" (More Than a Club), is central to the idea of being members-led, applying a democratic approach to an institution. Though we often hear from Barcelona's team president, they are not the owner of the club. Instead, they are a part-owner, who is elected by other owners, and elections are usually held every six years.

If you are not much into soccer, but more into football, the Green Bay Packers team works exactly the same. Shareholders are granted voting rights, an invitation to the corporation's annual meeting, and an opportunity to purchase exclusive shareholder-only merchandise. While shareholders don't actually manage the daily operations of the teams as a way of eliminating chaos, they can vote for the team's board of directors and executive committee.

It may seem odd for someone who is used to seeing traditional ownership structures in business and sports, but those who understand cooperativism would likely associate it with the same type of governance cooperatives have. Cooperatives are customer-centric and collaborative as a result of their ownership structure, which is basically a model in which an organization is owned by its customers. This definitely makes accountability much more important, the division of profits more equitable, and the organization more customer-focused because the customer-owners make decisions about the cooperative strategy during regular meetings. While traditional cooperativism has been around since the 1800s, we now see a new form of cooperativism on the rise through Web3 brought about by decentralized autonomous organizations (DAOs), which is the new governance of the world of Web3.

A DAO is a new kind of organizational structure built on the blockchain that is often described as a sort of "crypto co-op." In their purest form, DAOs are groups formed around a common purpose, like investing in startups, managing a stablecoin (coins attached to a reference asset), or buying a bunch of NFTs. ConsenSys, a blockchain organization, defines DAOs as "governing bodies that oversee the allocation of resources tied to the projects they are associated with and are also tasked with ensuring the long-term success of the project they support." Once formed, a DAO is run by its members, often through the use of tokens. These tokens generally come with certain rights attached, such as the ability to manage a common treasury or vote on certain decisions. These are utility tokens.

44

DAOs and their governance structure stem from the impact of smart contracts, which gave rise to trustless governance systems since there is no need for a middleman anymore. Although the word "trustless" might make you think trust is not needed, it is actually referring to the concept that there is no need to trust an intermediary anymore, since trust is replaced by technology.

With smart contracts, these organizations become autonomous, and DAO members participate with tokens, create proposals about the future of the DAO, and then come together to vote on each proposal. Proposals that achieve some predefined level of consensus are then accepted and enforced by the rules stated within the smart contract. Therefore, for a DAO to work, smart contracts, tokenization, and a voting system are necessary.

One of the main benefits of DAOs is that they maximize transparency by reducing the principal-agent problem affecting traditional business structures. This problem is based on the conflict in interests and priorities that arises when one person or entity is expected to take actions in the best interest of another party or entity. Problems like this can occur in business situations, with the most common one being in the relationship between a CEO and stakeholders. One example would be maximizing short-term profits in order to get a large bonus rather than focusing on the long-term sustainability of the business. In these cases, the agent (the CEO) may act in a way that does not align with the priorities and goals determined by the principal (the stakeholders) and, instead, act in their own self-interest.

DAOs solve this through community governance. Stakeholders aren't forced to join a DAO and only do so after understanding the rules governing it. They don't need to trust any agent acting on their behalf because they work as part of a group whose incentives are aligned. Stakeholders' interests align as the nature of a DAO incentivizes them not to be malicious. Since they have a stake in the network, they will want to see it succeed, and acting against it would be acting against their own self-interest.

There are many types of DAOs, including those that manage protocols, investment DAOs, and even collector's DAOs, such as the ConstitutionDAO, which was formed in 2021 to purchase an original copy of the US Constitution (although they raised $47 million dollars, the DAO eventually didn't make it as it was outbid by Ken Griffin, the founder of Citadel).

As a business, there are many benefits to launching or participating in a DAO, and DAOs can serve many purposes. You can set up a DAO in order to bring together investors in a startup, which would turn it into an investment DAO. You, as a participant investor, will have the opportunity to evaluate more investment opportunities since more DAO members will have the incentive to share the deals they are considering. You can also get access to bigger deals since you are pooling money with other DAOs members. DAOs are not only going to continue to grow and be important to businesses, but they are going to change the future of business altogether, as we will see more in Chapter 7.

Metaverse, Digital Twins, and Interoperability

Back in 2019, Kevin Kelly, founder of WIRED magazine, wrote a cover story titled "Welcome to the Mirrorworld," describing how augmented reality will unleash the next big tech platforms. He writes, "We are building a 1-to-1 world map of almost unimaginable reach. When completed, our physical reality will merge with the digital universe." In other words, get ready to meet your digital twin and the digital twin of your home, country, office, and even your life.

A digital twin is not a clone of ourselves but more of a digital replica of physical objects. They are actually virtual models designed to accurately reflect objects being studied. For example, a wind turbine is outfitted with various sensors related to vital areas of functionality, which produce data about different aspects of the physical object's performance, such as energy output, temperature, and weather conditions. This data is then relayed to a processing system and applied to the digital copy. Once informed with such data, the virtual model can be used to run simulations, study performance issues, and generate possible improvements. This is all done with the goal of generating valuable insights, which can then be applied back to the original physical object.

The truth is, this is not limited to physical objects – it applies to people too. In order to improve the accuracy of clinical trials, pharmaceutical company Merck KGaA is working with Unlearn.ai, a medical digital twin startup, to incorporate prognostic information from digital twins into its randomized controlled trials, which will enable smaller control groups and generate evidence suitable for supporting regulatory decisions in its immunology division. Clinical trials with FDA approval cost roughly $19 million dollars, according to Johns Hopkins data, so these simulations greatly reduce trial costs. Creating a digital twin of the patient before starting the trial and processing historical clinical trial datasets from patients to build "disease-specific" machine-learning models can be used to create digital twins with corresponding virtual medical records. These digital twins' records would be longitudinal, incorporating data over time and across systems, and cover demographic information, common test results, and biomarkers that look identical to actual patient records in a clinical trial.

Armed with all this, pharma companies can ensure the patient undergoing the trial can be compared to his or her own digital twin in the health simulation and not with another patient undergoing a placebo treatment. This makes the trial results much more accurate while reducing the required number of patients needed to be enrolled in the trials.

In Web3, the new interface is the metaverse. The term metaverse comes from the union of the Greek prefix *meta-*, meaning "beyond," and the word "universe." It is a shared virtual and collective space created by the convergence of two great spheres: a virtually-enhanced physical reality through augmented reality and a virtual space that duplicates the physical world through digital twins, made possible by the combination various of sensors, wearables, and devices that fall under the term Internet of Things (IoT) coupled with virtual reality (VR) technologies.

There are multiple metaverses, many of which are related to gaming, like Fortnite, Roblox, WoW, and Pokemon Go. There are also metaverses for socializing like Decentraland, The Sandbox, and Horizon Worlds. Then, there are industrial metaverses, where digital twins of physical equipment help manufacturing businesses run their operations more efficiently. When it comes to what is possible, the sky's the limit – we can have a health metaverse, dating metaverse, metaverses for work, and so on!

With so many different metaverses, navigating between them all can seem daunting. This is where an open metaverse, or a true metaverse, can remove some of those challenges. There are six characteristics that can make an open metaverse as impactful as the Internet itself, if not more. These six characteristics are:

1. Interoperability: Users can take out the value they created inside one platform and bring it to another platform, and vice versa, without any barriers.

2. Decentralized: On a blockchain, data becomes immutable, verifiable, and traceable, foregoing the need for a trusted

intermediary to manage the source of truth of the information at hand. Most metaverses today are centralized.

3. Persistent: Experiences, whether virtual or augmented, remain available and online for anyone who has access to it and for as long as the creator decides. They are available even when users aren't physically online.

4. Immersive: Spatial data will enable users to interact with digital items, whether placed in the virtual or real world, in the most natural way, using our five senses.

5. Community-led: Users can create unique, immersive brand experiences made with the community and potentially even controlled and owned by the community.

6. Self-sovereign: Users remain in control over their online identity and data, rather than the platform or website owning it.

Brands and companies have not shied away from the metaverse, and some are showing great results. Nike pioneered branding in the metaverse by launching sneakers in Fortnite and recently acquired a company called RTFKT that creates virtual, collectible sneakers for the metaverse. Nike also launched Nikeland in Roblox, which is having significant success, with almost seven-million people visiting its "micro metaverse" from 224 different countries, solidifying the fact that the metaverse can be a platform where the whole world can come together. As a way of trying to bring in more visitors, they brought LeBron James in during the NBA All-Star Weekend to interact with visitors inside the platform. Nike's CEO Jack Donahoe publicly admitted the importance of the metaverse for Nike in 2022, saying, "With Nike Virtual Studios (ex-RTFKT), our vision is to take our best-in-class experiences in digital and build Web3 products and experiences to scale this community so that Nike and our members can create, share, and benefit together."

Disney is also attributing many of its successes to their metaverse initiatives as digital experiences helped drive growth across the company. CEO Bob Chapek told analysts in a 2022 earnings call that the mix of physical and virtual experiences is also a priority for Disney moving forward. He said, "While multi-platform television and streaming will continue to be the foundation of sports coverage for the immediate future, we believe the opportunity for The Walt Disney Company goes well beyond these channels. It extends to sports betting, gaming, and the Metaverse." Disney also announced the appointment of Mike White to the role of SVP of Next Generation Storytelling, whose role will involve "connecting the physical and digital worlds," according to a press release.

At the same time, the immersive environment of the metaverse is not just an opportunity for consumer-facing companies. From training future surgeons to launching product demonstrations for retail salespeople, there are many B2B applications. Technology company Nvidia believes investing in manufacturing and logistics metaverse simulations will reduce waste and accelerate better business solutions, so they launched Nvidia Omniverse, a platform for businesses to create their own industrial metaverses. Digital twins also can be used to monitor and do maintenance of interconnected machinery from miles away from the plant and even from the comfort of your house or office.

At the same time, Microsoft is positioning its cloud computing services to be the fabric of the metaverse, using its Mesh platform to allow avatars and immersive spaces to be interconnected in collaborative environments like Teams. With remote or hybrid work environments, many of these more creative, virtual business experiences are likely to become even more relevant to how companies connect with their employees and customers.

AI and the Six Technology Enablers

I read the book *The Future is Faster Than You Think* by futurists Peter Diamantis and Steven Kotler in early 2020, and it dramatically changed my view of technology as it introduced me to the concept of technology convergence. They argue that profound technological shifts happen not because of the emergence of new technology but because of the unique combination of a number of them. By definition, technology convergence is the act of bringing previously unrelated technologies together, often in a single device or solution. Smartphones are one of the best possible examples of such convergence.

Prior to the widespread adoption of smartphones, consumers generally relied on a collection of single-purpose devices, such as telephones, wristwatches, digital cameras, and global positioning system (GPS) navigators. Today, even low-end smartphones combine the functionality of all these separate devices into a single device.

The technology convergence of blockchain, tokens, DAOs, and the metaverse all makeup Web3 as its four pillars. When they work together with AI, technology enablers allow Web3 to function. Because data is key as both the input and output of Web3, we will be overwhelmed with data, but the only way to have Web3 work is through data. This is why there are six main technology enablers related to the concept of data. Before we can understand the main technology enablers, we have to ask ourselves the following questions:

- How do we collect all this data?
- How do we protect it?
- How do we process it?
- How do we transmit it?
- How do we extract insights from it?
- How do we visualize it?

These questions are answered with the following six technology enablers:

1. Internet of Things (IoT)
2. Cryptography and hashing
3. Edge computing
4. 5G
5. AI and machine learning (ML)
6. Extended reality (XR), namely VR, AR, and MR.

You can see a graphical representation below:

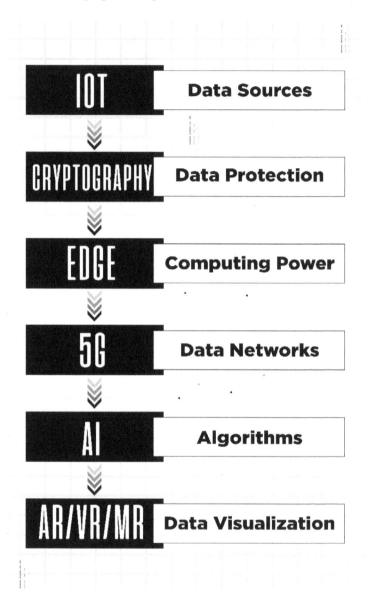

Let's start off with data collection. The Internet of Things (IoT) is a new concept related to data collection hardware. IoT can be defined as a giant network of physical objects, and even people, embedded with sensors, software, and other technologies for the purpose of connecting and exchanging data with other devices and systems over the Internet. These devices range from ordinary household objects to sophisticated industrial tools. With more than 14 billion IoT devices connected, all of these devices collect and share data about the way they are being used and the environment around them. The IoT is the key enabler of digital twins and the metaverse, as well as the data source that feeds the blockchain with updated information. There would be no Web3 without an ever-expanding network of the Internet of Things to feed Web3 with its most important raw data.

Once we collect the data, we need to protect it. Blockchain security is built on two concepts: cryptography and hashing. Cryptography is a method of securing data from unauthorized access. In the blockchain, cryptography is used to secure transactions taking place between two nodes in a blockchain network, and hashing is used to secure the block information and the linked blocks in a blockchain. Hashing enables immutability in the blockchain. The encryption in cryptographic hashing does not involve any use of keys or passwords. When a transaction is verified, the hash algorithm adds the hash to the block, and a new unique hash is added to the block from the original transaction. Hashing continues to combine or make new hashes, but the original footprint is still accessible. Innovations in these two areas have made it possible to make the blockchain an unhackable, transparent "ledger of truth."

Then, a new computing paradigm for processing all this data is reshaping the world of Web3 – edge computing. Edge refers to a range of networks and devices at or near the user. It's about processing data closer to where it's being generated, enabling processing at greater speeds and volumes, and leading to greater action-led results in real-time. Today, cloud computing is the most widespread paradigm, which allows enterprises to supplement their private data centers with global servers that extend their infrastructure to any location and scale computational resources as needed. But applications running in real-time throughout the world can require significant local processing power, often in remote locations too far from centralized cloud servers, and some workloads need to remain on-premise or in a specific location due to low latency (time delay) or data-residency requirements. While cloud processing does the work in a distant, centralized data reserve, edge computing handles and stores data locally in an edge device. Instead of being dependent on an internet connection, the device can operate as a standalone network node. Edge computing is necessary for IoT to work better and help decentralized blockchain nodes verify and store data faster.

Then, we have to know how to transmit data. The new network to process all this data is 5G, which will substitute 4G. 5G wireless technology is meant to deliver multiple GBs per second with peak data speeds, ultra-low latency, more reliability, massive network capacity, increased availability, and a more uniform user experience for more users. As any other wireless network, it uses radio frequencies, also known as spectrum technology, to carry information through the air, but 5G uses higher radio frequencies that are less cluttered, allowing us to carry more information at a much faster rate. 5G will enable widespread IoT usage and outperform 4G across all specifications, from download speeds between 10x to 20x times faster and exponentially lower latency. This will also enable more interoperability in the metaverse, faster blockchain processing, and no latency in digital twins management.

Artificial intelligence (AI) is the technology enabler that allows us to extract insights from the data. When it comes to extracting insights, we *need* to use technology because there is going to be too much data, and humans cannot process it all without the help of technology. To extract insight from all the data, AI combines computer science and robust datasets to enable problem-solving through algorithms that try to replicate human decision-making. It includes the subfields of machine learning and deep learning, which are frequently mentioned in conjunction with AI. These disciplines basically work out algorithms to make predictions or classifications based on input data.

Looking back to Gartner's Web3 pillars, one being the Semantic Web, this is where AI jumps in. Web3 envisions a digital realm where machines can communicate directly with other machines and users, but this requires machines to understand digital content in the first place. AI will become the cognitive layer of Web3 by providing deep learning algorithms and analytic capabilities to make machines "understand" online content. In essence, deep learning algorithms will train artificial intelligence to recognize different types of content and attribute meaning to them. This way, search engines won't just recommend the most popular type of content, but they will also have a basic understanding of it to help improve the overall user experience. In the end, the end customer will benefit. Some of the user-oriented benefits of applying AI as the cognitive layer of Web3 include better personalization and more responsive dApps and NFTs. Alethea AI's Alice is the first non-fungible token (NFT) with self-learning capabilities that changes how it interacts with people as it learns from every new interaction. As the first intelligent NFT (iNFT), Alice comes with her own personality and is capable of having exhaustive conversations with internet users and learning from them in the process.

We visualize all this data through what we can call extended reality (XR), which is an umbrella term to describe new technologies such as virtual reality (VR), mixed reality (MR), and augmented reality (AR).

• Virtual Reality (VR) is an immersive experience deemed as a computer-simulated reality. It refers to computer technologies using reality headsets to generate realistic sounds, images, and other sensations to imitate a real environment or create an imaginary world. Think of the content you can interact with through the Oculus Quest by Facebook.

- Augmented Reality (AR) is a live, direct, or indirect view of a physical, real-world environment whose elements are augmented, or supplemented, by computer-generated sensory input such as sound, video, graphics, or GPS data. AR utilizes your existing reality and adds to it by utilizing a device of some sort. Mobile devices and tablets are the most popular mediums of AR now. Through the camera, apps like SnapChat and PokemonGo put an overlay of digital content into the environment.

- Mixed Reality (MR), sometimes referred to as hybrid reality, is the merging of real and virtual worlds to produce new environments and visualizations where physical and digital objects coexist and interact in real-time. It means placing new imagery within a real space in such a way that the new imagery can interact, to an extent, with what is real in the physical world we know. The key characteristic of MR is that the synthetic content and the real-world content are able to react to each other in real-time, almost as an immersive AR, no longer tied to a limited screen or viewer. For instance, NASA partnered with Microsoft to create the software OnSight to help scientists and engineers be virtually present on Mars while still being physically on Earth.

Together, these six technologies converge to create Web3, as they lay the foundations of the four main pillars of Web3 with blockchain as its data layer, tokens as its goods and currencies, DAOs as its new governance, and the metaverse as its interface. These new concepts and technologies are so transformative that they change the whole business context, or *zeitgeist*, by making some leadership duties and responsibilities obsolete and unnecessary because technology performs them better. At the same time, other leadership responsibilities become increasingly more important. This is why leaders will need to develop new skills and become meta-leaders in the world of AI and Web3.

Andrea Iorio

CHAPTER 3:

Reperception

Imagine yourself as a famous detective working on an important case in which a valuable work of art was stolen. As a successful detective, you're confident the owner of the painting is guilty. Even though he was the first to call 911, he was acting very strange when asked about his whereabouts throughout the day. When asked where the painting was before it disappeared, he gave a somewhat confusing response. At the same time, you find out he raised his insurance premium a few weeks before the theft. Given this evidence, you consider him to be the prime suspect. However, after a few days, the forensic team returned with evidence of someone else's fingerprints at the crime scene, and surveillance camera footage surfaced, showing a hooded man entering the house at night while no one was home. As a detective, what do you do?

Do you continue to investigate the owner because of past evidence, or do you update your suspect list based on new evidence?

If you're truly a good detective, you would re-evaluate your suspicions in the face of new evidence. This doesn't necessarily mean the owner of the painting is no longer at fault, though. After all, he could have simply hired someone to steal it from him so he could collect the insurance money. But if you don't update your perceptions in this case and at least investigate the second suspect, you would be guilty of negligence as a detective.

The truth is, the same applies to many other situations in life and business. Think of a doctor who doesn't change their prescription for a patient after a new blood test shows their first diagnosis was wrong, or the current treatment is not working. Imagine a construction company discovering the land they are halfway through building a skyscraper on is being built on is dangerous terrain. What if, despite this new evidence, the engineers decide to continue the project simply because they didn't want all of their work to go to waste?

You might be thinking *that would be crazy*, and you're right! These actions would be considered unethical and possibly even criminal.

Yet, somehow, we are guilty of doing this in our businesses all the time. We are constantly being presented with new evidence, but we fail to update our way of thinking, our systems, and our processes, only to maintain the good old status quo because it's comfortable and it's what we know. Our natural human tendency to fall back into our old habits will affect our ability, as leaders, to navigate the world of Web3, which is why meta-leaders will need to develop reperception.

Reperception is a term originally used by Amy Webb, the founder of Future Today Institute, at SXSW 2022. While I was in the audience listening, she defined reperception as "the ability to see, hear, or become aware of something new in existing information. Noticing what others missed." Reperception is best understood with an experiment. Look carefully at the image below. What do you see?

People might see different things in it, but the truth is, there *is* a correct answer. In 1951, the Board of the University of Illinois performed an experiment in which many research participants were shown the same dotted, black-and-white image above. Initially, no one saw anything in the image. Then, participants started seeing different objects, ranging from maps to different animals. After receiving the initial feedback from their participants, the researchers informed the participants it was a cow. Yes, a cow. Can you see it now?

Initially, everyone was surprised, but the more they stared at the image, the more they could see the cow once they had this new information. They even felt kind of stupid for not having seen it to begin with. Interestingly enough, once they saw the image of the cow, they couldn't unsee it. In other words, they formed a new perception of the image and could no longer return to their previous perception.

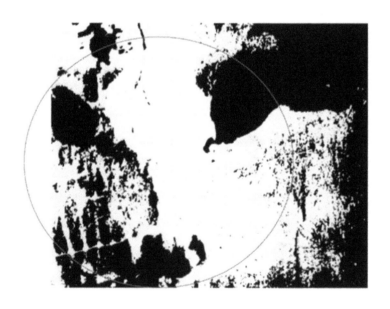

In an exponentially changing world, the ability to see, hear, or become aware of new information is one of the greatest skills meta-leaders of today need to lead their companies through Web3. What may have worked in your business yesterday is unlikely to bring you success tomorrow in a world that is constantly changing. When we let go of our past beliefs, we make room to absorb new knowledge and reformulate our view of the world and our business. This requires you to think critically about new problems arising in your industry and solve them through constant reinvention without waiting for others to solve them before you do.

Let's look at a concrete example in the aerospace industry. The biggest bottleneck in the industry has traditionally been the cost of the rocket – not just the cost of the rocket itself, but the fact that each rocket could only be launched once since they didn't have landing technology. Each mission requires engineers to build a completely new rocket, as well as a new launch pad. These costs have created a huge barrier to increasing the number of space missions, as well as private space exploration projects. Elon Musk, founder and CEO of SpaceX, spent years trying to innovate technology to make it cheaper for people to go to space using commercial flights. To break this bottleneck, Musk had three options:

1. Buy cheaper rockets from countries like Russia or China, which would allow them to increase their fleet at a cheaper cost.

2. Marginally and consistently improve the efficiency of SpaceX's operations to reduce the production costs of the rocket.

3. Rethink the entire rocket engineering and internally develop an innovative landing solution for the rockets, allowing them to be reusable.

The simple solution would have been to pursue one of the first two options. But we know Elon Musk chose the third, which transformed the aerospace industry in December 2015 when SpaceX successfully landed a Falcon 9 rocket in Cape Canaveral, Florida. With Falcon 9, SpaceX has proven and popularized the concept of launching and vertically landing a rocket. Although the Falcon 9 is smaller and has less capacity than NASA's space shuttle, it costs substantially less than other models, with research showing that the Falcon 9 is 10x cheaper than NASA's space shuttles.

This type of innovation wasn't possible with conventional linear thinking. Instead, it required critical thinking, which is the catalyst for reperception. "What if I could land a rocket?" might have sounded like a dumb question to all the seasoned executives from the aerospace industry, but it contained the critical thinking necessary to reperceive the future of the industry.

The same happened at Filmr, an app co-founded by Ricardo and Fernando Whately, in which I was an early investor. In a market where all video editing apps followed a horizontal pattern, inherited from desktop editing software like Adobe's Premiere, Filmr challenged the status quo by proposing a vertical editing timeline that made more sense on a smartphone, ensuring better usability. If we had looked at it in comparison to what we have always done, we would have fought other editing apps in the horizontal format without a clear competitive advantage. Today, Filmr is the only editor on the market with a vertical timeline. Of course, we were afraid to position ourselves differently from everyone else, but it paid off. In addition to being considered one of the Best Apps of 2019 by Apple, Filmr was sold in early 2021 to InVideo, an Indian company. In a way, all we had to do was turn the screen and ask, "How could we do it differently?"

We cannot copy and paste our past successes and past beliefs in a world that is constantly changing. To avoid falling prey to this, we must practice a beginner's mindset, which is a Buddhist concept used to describe an open mind free of any preconceptions. It's a clean slate. Many centuries ago, a professor asked a Zen master to teach him the meaning of life. The master silently started to pour tea into a cup. Even when the cup was full, he continued to pour, and the tea started to spill over. The professor could not hold back any longer and impatiently asked, "Master, why do you keep pouring the tea even though the cup is full?"

The master replied, "I want to show you your mind is like this cup, so full that nothing can be added. You must first empty your mind of prejudices and past knowledge before trying to understand the meaning of life."

A beginner's mindset is like the mind of a five-year-old. Studies show that children at this age ask around 100-300 questions per day. It might seem like asking questions at this age is child's play, but it's not. The simple behavior of asking questions is a sign of a complex level of reasoning, which first requires an understanding of what we don't know, then an effort to do something to make up for it. This type of reasoning activates brain regions linked to reward systems, and our reward is added knowledge. This type of elaborate thinking cannot be done by machines, which means, in the world of digital transformation, a child in early development exercises critical thinking better than AI.

Human reasoning is not just about logically combining existing knowledge to come up with a solution or critique of a problem. It is also about reasoning beyond the universe of current knowledge and using imagination to form new ideas, whereas artificial intelligence can only look for solutions from its current set of existing knowledge.

Centuries after the Zen master's story above, the Buddhist monk Shunryu Suzuki said, "If your mind is empty, it is ready for anything; it is open to anything. In the beginner's mind, there are many possibilities, but in the expert's mind, there are few." Ironically, this Buddhist concept has never been more relevant than it is today in the midst of digital transformation, where the speed with which technology changes is faster than we ever thought possible.

Imagine being able to track the exact location of any product your business sells in real-time. If you are the leader of a shampoo manufacturing company, you may discover a manufacturing error in a certain batch of your shampoos that is giving customers a horrible side effect. The thousands of bottles of shampoo in that particular batch were already sold last month to your distributors. Your distributors have already resold them all to their smaller retailers in their region, and the smaller retailers have already sold all the products to their end customers. In fact, there have been so many advertisements on Amazon for this shampoo by third parties that it's possible for some of these shampoos to have been resold by the end customer to other consumers.

As a leader, it is your responsibility to track all the products in this batch quickly. But let's face it, your first thought is that it's impossible to do this in a timely way, so you might as well think of a plan B, and if that doesn't work, a plan C. This way of thinking disregards the possibility that we can know, in real-time, who the consumers are from the outset. In the world of Web3, leaders should not even think like that because as transactions between customers are carried out using the blockchain, they will know exactly who has the products in real-time and be able to notify the customers directly for recall.

If you think this scenario is simply an episode of the Netflix series *Black Mirror*, depicting a hypothetical future dominated by technology, you are wrong. In 2016, the Vice President of Food Safety at Walmart asked his team to trace a package of sliced mangoes to the farmer who picked them. It took his team 6 days, 18 hours, and 26 minutes. While all the data was in their system, arriving at the information took a long time. But after partnering with IBM to create a food traceability system based on Hyperledger Fabric, a project hosted by the Linux Foundation, Walmart could trace the mangoes stored in its US stores within 2.2 seconds – literally, at the speed of thought.

Consider another question – If a tree falls and hits a 5G antenna in Stockholm, does it make noise in Chicago? Thanks to Ericsson building urban-scale digital twins on the Nvidia Omniverse platform to help accurately simulate the interaction between a 5G infrastructure and the environment for maximum performance and coverage, we now know the answer is yes. Everything from the location of trees to the height and composition of buildings is crucial because they impact 5G wireless signals on networks serving smartphones, tablets, and millions of other internet-connected devices.

The world of AI and Web3 is going to break down past beliefs and show us new evidence all the time. But if, as leaders, we don't have the skill of reperception, we will be stuck, inflexible, in the face of these changes. It's no longer the leader's ability to perceive that matters; it's their ability to reperceive by constantly rethinking and relearning. What was a good decision yesterday will not be the best decision tomorrow, so leaders need to rethink their decisions all the time in the face of new information and exponential changes.

However, this is not to say we have to constantly change our minds to keep up with the changes happening around us. Too much reperception can also be detrimental to ourselves and our businesses. We need to find a balance between being open-minded and having a clear long-term vision and principles to guide our decision-making.

One of the biggest challenges with reperception is that, as humans, our brains naturally resist rethinking and reprogramming. We are influenced by external factors and mechanisms that make us think by default and limit our ability to exercise critical thinking. Four main phenomena prevent us from thinking critically and practicing reperception:

1. Confirmation bias: This is the idea that we shape the information we obtain according to our view of the world, and we tend to seek information with which we agree. In other words, we look for new information that confirms what we already know.

2. Information bottleneck: This phenomenon states that there is often so much new information to process that we cannot look clearly at the information in front of us, causing us to become indecisive or make wrong decisions. This is best described by the "paradox of choice" effect, which suggests an abundance of options requires more effort to choose and can leave us feeling unsatisfied with our choice.

3. Path dependence: This concept explains that we make decisions about the future based on our past successes. We tend to follow the same steps, and make the same decisions we made in the past because they are familiar and comfortable. Replicating our past successes might work in an analog, linear world, but unfortunately, it does not work in the current rapidly changing environment.

4. Ego: The biggest enemy to reperception is one that made the title of a famous Harvard Business Review article called "Ego is the Enemy of Good Leadership." As we move up the hierarchy, we acquire more power, and with power, people are likely to want to please us more, agree with us more (and even laugh at our jokes!), which reinforces our belief that our vision is correct.

Reperception, more often than not, requires us to challenge our own identity. Admitting we were wrong may sound easy, but it's not. It requires us to face the reality that one of our beliefs is wrong, and then we have to openly admit we are capable of being wrong. Some leaders let pride get in the way, and many leaders worry being wrong is a sign of weakness and that their team will lose trust in them. In reality, it's the exact opposite. It takes strength to admit fault, and teams will respect you more for it. When we admit we're wrong, a weight is suddenly lifted from our minds, like telling the truth after holding back a lie. It's not just liberating; it's valuable too. No longer burdened by the need to be right, we have the chance to learn something new and understand the world better.

In organizational psychologist Adam Grant's book *Think Again*, Grant recalls a lecture he once gave, unaware that Daniel Kahneman, one of the greatest social scientists of all time, was in the audience. At the end of his lecture, Adam Grant came down from the stage and saw Kahneman. Kahneman's eyes lit up brightly as he said, "That was wonderful. I was wrong."

This strange and contradictory sentence intrigued Grant since most of the time, we hear people say, "That was wonderful. I was right," or "You were wrong, and let me tell you why." Grant asked Kahneman to sit down with him and explain his reaction.

Kahneman said, "Nobody likes to be wrong, but I like to have been wrong because it means I'm less wrong now than I was before."

Most people do not have this optimistic reaction to being wrong, but Kahneman rejoices in being wrong, even when his core beliefs are attacked or threatened. When Grant asked him why and how he can rejoice under such circumstances, Kahneman said, "Finding out I was wrong is the only way to be sure I learned something."

He further explains by connecting beliefs to attachments. There are good ideas everywhere, but our attachment to them is tentative. Kahneman doesn't fall in love with these ideas, and they don't become part of his identity. Ideas are simply hypotheses, and hypotheses are not always accurate. More often than not, they are wrong or incomplete. The ability to let go of these ideas and separate them from our identity is what makes a good thinker and a good leader. A good leader needs to have this ability to reperceive because the changes Web3 technologies have introduced in the business world are so profound and sudden that the certainty of any idea will be short-lived.

Aside from the ego, another challenge in reperception is the fact that while technology evolves exponentially, human beings still think linearly. We live in an era of new discoveries and rapid changes, unlike any other era. What makes this moment particularly unique is these changes are happening at a speed difficult for our brains to comprehend, graphically represented by a mathematical expression not often found in nature: an exponential curve. Our minds have been conditioned to think about growth and change in linear terms because that's what we're familiar with. Think about how we age, one year at a time. Think about how a tree grows as new branches sprout, slowly and predictably. We are not used to seeing situations where things change gradually, then suddenly at an unexpected speed. But while humans are linear, technologies evolve exponentially.

Legend has it that the creator of chess gave this new game as a gift to an emperor in India. Impressed by the ingenuity of the game, the emperor felt obliged to give the man a reward and asked the creator what he would like in return. The man humbly replied, "Oh, Emperor, my wishes are simple. I only wish this: give me one grain of rice for the first square of the chessboard, two grains for the next square, four for the next, eight for the next, and so on, for all 64 squares, with each square having twice the number of grains in the previous square."

The emperor was surprised that this resourceful man only wanted a few grains of rice as a reward for such a wonderful game. Without much thought, he granted the man his wish. Sometime later, the emperor's treasurer returned and warned the emperor it would be impossible to pay the man the amount requested, as the rice amounted to an astronomical total, far more than his empire could produce in many, many centuries.

How could the emperor be so easily deceived? It's simple – he was thinking linearly, as most of us tend to do, while the resourceful man understood and used the power of exponentiality. Here lies the threat or the opportunity, depending on your point of view. Humans tend to think linearly, but the technological changes we are experiencing right now follow an exponential curve. This is why we, as meta-leaders, need to rethink much more than we think and continuously reperceive what we think we know.

CHAPTER 4:

Data Sensemaking

Imagine yourself at the grocery store on a Monday morning in the cereal aisle, and you have to choose which cereal is healthiest for you. You've been focusing more on your health lately, and you're determined to lose weight by eating better. But imagine doing this manually, without using technology or the Internet. You have to go item by item, brand by brand, reading ingredient by ingredient, examining nutritional information one after another, and making your decision based on the data you've gathered. Would that be efficient?

Definitely not. You'd be lucky enough to make it home by dinner, let alone breakfast.

This process is inefficient because it includes analyzing too much data and takes too much time to process, which is harmful to decision-making processes.

Data is a double-edged sword. Just as making decisions without data is terrible, so is making decisions with too much data. Without data, the decision-making process is based on guesswork and intuition only, a bit like it was in the analog world. Too much data can also hold us back in the decision-making process because it overwhelms us, taking our focus away from what is important. According to Barry Schwartz, author of *The Paradox of Choice*, having too many options available causes us to make worse decisions. In the situation of choosing a cereal, you're unlikely to make the best decision in the face of over 100 options, all with varying nutritional information.

We already live in a world with lots and lots of data. More than 90% of the data generated since the beginning of humanity was generated in the last decade, and we hit 97 zettabytes of data by the end of 2022, according to Statista. A zettabyte is a number with 12 zeros behind it – so that's a lot of data! It is so much data that Brazilian data scientist and my great friend Ricardo Cappra created the term "infoxication" to define the information overload or intoxication we experience as a result of the overwhelming data and the difficulty in managing it.

But this current volume of data is nothing compared to what is coming. In the world of Web3, we will be able to measure everything from the movement of our customer's hand picking up a product to the speed at which an item drops from our highest shelf and even the intensity of the vibration of a refrigerator that contains expensive wines. We will have exactly the same problem as we had with the cereal selection – too much data at hand.

In the Web3 world, where everything is measurable, data will become a commodity, and the real challenge for leaders will be choosing the metrics to be monitored and prioritized, then extracting insights from them by "making sense" of all this data. The choice of these metrics and the correlations between them will bring about innovative insights your competition may not even be looking at, leading to a competitive advantage for the leaders and companies able to practice data sensemaking, which is a new skill required of a meta-leader.

Sensemaking, a term introduced by Karl Weick, refers to how we structure the unknown to be able to act in it. Sensemaking involves coming up with a plausible understanding – a map – of a shifting world; testing this map with others through data collection, action, and conversation; then refining or abandoning the map depending on how credible it is. This concept becomes more complex as new information is collected and new actions are taken. Then, as patterns are identified, and new information is labeled and categorized, the complex becomes simple once again, but with a higher level of understanding.

When we put this into the complex context of big data, where we live so much of our lives online, it's never been easier for companies to access real behavioral data about what people do, when they do it, how they do it, and how often they do it.

Big, quantitative data can answer these questions in real-time, based on observed data rather than survey data. This has ultimately revolutionized market research in the past decade.

In an analog world, we relied on survey data and simply asked the customer what they wanted, but customers don't always know what they want, which is why data sensemaking is more reliable. In 2006, Steve Jobs held focus groups at Apple to understand which type of smartphone customers wanted. When asked, the majority of people wanted a smartphone with a big screen and a big keyboard, which was just a bigger and better version of a Blackberry, the market leader at the time. No one asked for a touchscreen phone without a keyboard. If Steve Jobs had taken that feedback and followed it, the iPhone wouldn't have launched in 2007, and the majority of Apple innovations we have today wouldn't exist. Innovators and leaders are not responsible for responding to customers' requests and wishes. Instead, they should anticipate their customers' needs without those needs being expressed, and the only way to do that is through data sensemaking.

In my first days as the Head of Tinder in Latin America, I created a dashboard showing the main metrics, which included the number of downloads, active users, swipes, matches, and so on. I was updating the numbers every day and making ongoing decisions based on the current data, certain it would help me make better decisions. But it didn't. Knowing the absolute number of downloads yesterday wasn't helping me make any innovative or assertive decisions today. Only once I started looking at percentages – the increases and decreases of these metrics over time – I began making better decisions for the company. If I noticed a decrease in the number of downloads throughout the week, I used this data as a starting point for my decisions on how much to invest in marketing. Even though this was better than simply looking at absolute numbers, it also didn't guarantee a continuous increase over time or explain why the trend was happening.

Determined to solve this problem and this blindness in managing Tinder, despite having a lot of data at hand, I started to experiment with non-obvious correlations between the obvious metrics and created a new metric called "degree of user self-esteem." This new metric was the percentage of matches for each "like" users gave while swiping on Tinder. If you're unfamiliar with how Tinder works, here is a brief overview. In order to chat with someone on Tinder, you have to "like" that person first, and that person has to "like" you back. Once you both "like" each other, it becomes a "match," and the app will allow you to chat. I discovered that users who had one match for every two likes they gave felt empowered and had a heightened sense of self-esteem, which increased their likelihood of spending more time in the app and feeling more satisfied with their experience. On the other hand, if users only received one match out of every ten likes, they would feel frustrated and unwanted, causing them to feel less satisfied and discontinue using the app. Based on the analysis of this metric by city, demographic, and user profile, I was able to clearly define my marketing and investment strategy.

There is an enormous difference between data, information, and insights. All too often, the terms data and information are used interchangeably, but they don't mean the same thing. Data is raw material. It is rough, uncut, unfiltered, and unrefined, like a freshly mined diamond. Computers have no problem working with millions of rows of unsorted data in the most basic form of ones and zeroes, which are seemingly incomprehensible to the human eye. For us, data alone means nothing in and of itself. Once the data is processed and put into context, the result is information fit for human consumption. The information contains meaning and context so that we can understand its purpose and implications. Then, insights are the result of correlations between, or among, information.

To understand the difference between data, information, and insights, let's use GPS as an example, which starts as data received from positioned satellites. Assuming you have no knowledge of mapping coordinates, GPS reference numbers wouldn't tell you much about where you are located. Take the coordinates 44°20'42" N latitude and 8°32'48" longitude. Without entering them into Google, do you know what place in the world corresponds to these coordinates? Of course not. You would have to memorize the coordinates for every place on Earth. Spoiler – it's Celle Ligure, the village in Italy where I grew up. However, if you open Google Maps, that GPS reference point will be transformed into a pin on a map. This is information humans can understand.

When data becomes information, it becomes more palatable to us, but information alone does not give us a reference point for use in broader analyses. The map pin doesn't tell us how to find the nearest ATM without further processing, nor does it report how many traffic accidents have occurred at a particular intersection during the past year unless we actively solicit the information. These are the insights we need to make better decisions. So, even though we believe "the more data, the better," the secret is in how we use the data and the insights we aim to unveil.

We decide which insights we want to extract from the data. Knowing where the closest ATM is might be relevant to one person, but someone who only uses a credit card wouldn't benefit from this insight. Similarly, knowing how far the best seafood restaurant is from one person might not be the best insight to extract for someone who is highly allergic to shellfish. In business, it is the leader's responsibility to pick the most important metrics to be monitored and extract unique insights from them. This can prove to be a very strong competitive advantage for the meta-leader.

Like anything in business, there is always a cost, especially if we aren't able to make sense of data. Even though the iPhone had already launched in 2007, Blackberry was still the market leader in 2010, having 40% of the US market and 20% of the world market, which was really impressive. Even though the number of Blackberry users increased by almost ten times (from 8 million devices to 77 million) from 2007 to 2012, their market share dropped dramatically from over 50% to less than 10%. By mainly looking at internal metrics, which were positive and showed steady year-on-year growth, the Blackberry leadership team did not realize they were growing slower than the market was growing due to the widespread adoption of the iPhone. Because they were unable to make sense of their data, Blackberry eventually lost their competitive advantage to Apple.

As leaders, we don't often use data in the best ways for our business or our teams. In a report titled "The Experience of Work: The Role of Technology in Productivity and Engagement," published in 2020 by Oxford Economics in collaboration with SAP, only 55% of executives reported making data-driven decisions, and only 43% reported making real-time decisions. Hierarchical structures also represent a huge hurdle. Decision-making must be distributed across the organization, not concentrated to a few people in the executive team. According to a Forrester study, for every hour a product team spends on work, another 48 minutes is wasted waiting for decisions to be made. This equates to more than 3.5 hours of "wait time" in an average eight-hour workday. Some level of optimization is possible if we can make the decision-making process more agile by eliminating silos within companies, where one team doesn't speak to another, and parallel processing, which is more than one person making the same decision without discussion with each other. This must be combined with investments in technology to facilitate the accessibility of the information needed for the final decision.

When it comes to innovating and generating more customer value in the world of Web3, the competitive advantage for leaders and organizations won't come from accessing data but from choosing the metrics to monitor and prioritize to make ongoing decisions on top of the insights generated. According to a report by Credit Suisse, the metaverse will exponentially boost data generation by up to 20 times worldwide by 2032. In an exclusive interview for this book, Or Lenchner, CEO of

Bright Data, said, "It is easy to estimate that the amount of data and public web data will multiply several times over. According to recent estimates, by 2025, we expect online shopping and e-commerce to account for almost a quarter of all retail sales on some continents – and that will undoubtedly count for a lot of layers of data – mostly public web data."

Today, when you look at the metrics measured within any company, you will almost always find the same ones: month-to-month and year-to-year sales results, inventory, customer history, customer avatars, customer acquisition cost (CAC), customer lifetime value (CLV), and so on. Different companies in different industries are all looking at the same metrics, and while the difference often lies in the depth of the data, its quality, and how up-to-date it is, interestingly enough, their dashboards are almost identical.

Imagine if companies were military jets, their leaders were Air Force pilots competing in a race to hit a very critical target, and they were all looking at the same panels in the cockpit. This only allows them to differentiate themselves to a certain extent when it comes to flying their plane because it will be difficult to get such unique and differentiated insights if they are looking at the same dashboard. But if a pilot extends their control panel to look at totally different indicators based on future expectations or external trends, they open up the range of possibilities for differentiation and competitive advantage, as well as increase the likelihood of hitting that target.

This is a leadership and skillset issue. Bright Data research indicates 89% of businesses understand that even before the introduction of the metaverse actually happens, there lies a need to upskill and hire new staff and data-skilled employees to prepare for the new reality. In a world of Web3 and huge data, the great competitive advantage is no longer access to data but the ability to choose the most indicative metrics of future behaviors or customer demands, allowing us to make more predictive decisions rather than reactive ones.

Jorn Lyssegen, the founder of the social media monitoring platform Meltwater, used the metaphor of driving a car by looking in the rearview mirror to describe today's leaders in his book *Outside Insight*. He explains that, as leaders, we manage our companies as if we were driving a car, but instead of looking through the front window, we look through the rearview mirror. The front window shapes a vision of the future through correlations between external metrics and real-time data, while the rearview mirror only shows the internal metrics from the past. Inevitably, we will go slower, in zigzags, and sooner or later, we will crash the car.

Even for the best leaders, making sense of so much data can be challenging because it is simply too hard for any human or team to process it all and extract insights from it. This is where technology, particularly AI, can support us. The more we can outsource the tasks of processing and extracting insights from this huge volume of data generated in the world of Web3 to AI technologies, the better the leaders will be able to make sense of all this data.

AI and big data have a synergistic relationship. AI requires a massive scale of data to learn and improve decision-making processes, and big data analytics leverage AI for better data analysis. With this convergence, you can more easily leverage advanced analytic capabilities, like augmented or predictive analytics, and more efficiently surface actionable insights from your vast stores of data.

The abilities of AI continue to grow, and it can complete many of the tasks we are incapable of doing or don't have the time to do. It can identify data types, find possible connections among datasets, and recognize insights using natural language processing. It can be used to automate and accelerate data preparation tasks, including the generation of data models, and assist in data exploration. It can learn common human error patterns, detecting and resolving potential flaws in information. It can also learn by watching how the user interacts with an analytics program, quickly surfacing unexpected insights from massive datasets. AI can also learn subtle differences in meaning or context-specific nuances to help users better understand numeric data sources. In addition, AI can alert users to anomalies or unexpected patterns in data, actively monitoring events and identifying potential threats from system logs or social networking data.

According to data from International Data Corporation, approximately 30% of the world's data volume is being generated by the healthcare industry as of 2022. By 2025, the compound annual growth rate of data for healthcare will reach 36%, which is 6% faster than manufacturing, 10% faster than financial services, and 11% faster than media and entertainment. It's safe to say that health sector stakeholders, such as hospitals, doctors, and health insurance providers, are overwhelmed with the data they receive from wearable devices and IoT sensors. The latest Samsung phones are equipped with oximeters to measure our oxygen levels, earbuds can assess our core temperature, smart socks can monitor a baby's heart rate, and a sports bra can detect cancer. With all of these innovations, it is certain healthcare technology will literally touch us all on a daily basis, one day very soon.

As consumer wearables increasingly converge with medical technology, the rise of comfortable, patient-friendly devices will increase customer compliance and improve data collection. The next advancements will do more than just collect data; they will also suggest solutions and provide treatment. From a ring that promotes deeper sleep to insoles that help improve your stride, technology is quickly personalizing healthcare on a massive scale.

With the predictive power of AI, all of this data will help move the current health sector away from a reactive, sick-care approach, where intervention happens only after symptoms arise, to a much more proactive, value-based healthcare focused on the prevention of chronic diseases. For instance, multiple sclerosis (MS), a chronic disease affecting the central nervous system, is very hard to diagnose because there is no single test or finding on an exam to support the diagnosis. The disease can cause a number of different symptoms, which are likely to be treated by separate specialists, such as walking difficulties addressed by an orthopedist or visual blurring with occasional double vision treated by an ophthalmologist. Taken individually, these symptoms can be related to a very wide array of diseases much less serious than MS, but through the correlation of these symptoms, it might be much easier and faster to predict the chances of a patient developing MS, making it possible to treat it in its earlier stages.

If our medical data is shared by doctors in the form of an NFT and made available on the blockchain to stakeholders in the health sector, AI would be the tool to help diagnose us more efficiently by extracting probabilities from the health data at hand. C. Light Technologies, a neurotech and AI company, has developed an eye-tracking technology paired with machine learning that can be used to detect MS. C. Light's machine learning algorithms and instruments have the potential to allow for earlier and more accurate prognosis of MS, leading to better patient outcomes and reduced overall healthcare costs.

Like good Air Force pilots, leaders in the era of AI and Web3 will be the ones who get involved deeply in identifying and picking the metrics to be considered. They will constantly be redesigning the cockpits, so their teams can make their most predictive and innovative decisions, taking advantage of the enormous granularity of data coming from the metaverse. While this is excellent input for better decisions, it can become an obstacle if we do not know how to process and prioritize it in the right way.

This doesn't only apply to internal data. Companies that can externally support their clients and partners with data and allow their leaders to practice better sensemaking are growing in value and among the best performers in the market. John Deere is the largest farm equipment company in the world, with roots dating back to 1837 when a blacksmith named John Deere developed the first commercially successful self-scouring steel plow. Deere & Co. has grown into an industrial behemoth, selling nearly $50 billion worth of equipment. No longer just a one-plow product, the company produces and sells Deere tractors, lawnmowers, harvesters, tree cutters, specialized golf course mowers, and much more. If anything needs to be chopped, cut, mowed, sprayed, or moved, John Deere has a machine for it.

Beyond equipment, they generate much more value for farmers by providing data, up to the point of becoming a company that sells IoT equipment for precision agriculture. Beyond those bright green and yellow tractors plowing across a field of crops, these pieces of machinery are part of an IoT network for precision agriculture, where an intricate ecosystem of data flows across machines, farmers, John Deere, and external partners. Farms are ripe with valuable data to be harvested. To maximize yield potential, farmers must consider a myriad of variables including weather, timing, soil quality, moisture levels, nutrient levels, seed placement, frequency and dosage of fertilizer, and pesticide application. Over the past two-plus decades, Deere has been transforming from a pure equipment manufacturer into a data-driven technology company to deliver more value to farmers, helping them to collect data and harness it for improved farm management. The value created for farmers is improved productivity, increased efficiency, and reduced costs to ultimately maximize profitability.

Data, including crop management data and machine operation data (fuel level, location, machine hours, and engine RPM), is collected primarily from sensors embedded in both the machines and the soil of the fields. It is also pulled from external sources, such as weather prediction data and commodity pricing. Through telematics, the data is then automatically uploaded onto the cloud via cellular network, Wi-Fi, or Bluetooth. Farmers can access and manage the data through the MyJohnDeere.com portal of the cloud software platform. Through the operation center on this platform, farmers can then monitor activity in real-time, analyze performance, determine how best to utilize their equipment, collaborate with partners for insights, and provide prescriptions using algorithms to help the farmer decide what to plant, as well as where and when to plant it with optimized conditions. This type of softwarization of physical businesses leads to more efficient data generation and provides opportunities for meta-leaders to practice data sensemaking.

CHAPTER 5:

Cognitive Flexibility

Before the Internet, people could lie about themselves whether they met you at a bar or at work, but it wasn't easy to lie at scale. Digitalization opened those doors, allowing people to create fake identities on social media and dating apps. When I was the Head of Tinder in Latin America, this quickly became a safety concern on our app. I was faced with the dilemma of balancing user data privacy and the need to make the Tinder experience as safe as possible. This dilemma kept me up at night, as I asked myself if we were responsible for guaranteeing our users really were who they claimed to be. Because of the threat to our users' safety, I asked myself if we would be accountable if someone threatened the well-being of our users because we provided a platform for these two individuals to meet. Believe me, there were many unfortunate situations like that where I was questioned by local authorities to disclose the real identity of users who may have committed crimes, but I just had no way of doing that. At the time, there was no technology out there to help me guarantee the digital identity of users matched their physical ones, so this wasn't a dilemma I could solve using Web 2.0 technology.

The fact that people could reinvent themselves or create entirely new identities on social media was one of the criticisms during the rise of Web 2.0. We've all witnessed it – a couple on the verge of divorce posting photos with captions of how happy they are together or a college student posting about all the parties they go to on the weekend when, in reality, they have very few friends and spend most of their nights alone in their dorm. "Your life is not as great as you make it out to be on social media," became a common phrase, and it's still used today. The term "catfishing," which means creating a fake identity online to exploit others, became part of our vocabulary during this time as well.

The truth is, people today who are operating with Web 2.0 already have digital identities that do not match their real-world, offline identities. Now, imagine what identities are going to look like in the world of Web3 and the metaverse. Besides having several digital identities across multiple metaverses for work, play, and socialization, we will be the sole owners of our personal data and accounts based on the concepts of self-sovereign identity (SSI). This means no intermediary will have access to our data, but the data stored on the blockchain will be proof of an association between identities and a user.

At the same time, we need to consider the impact technologies have on the world today and on business. We often think about these impacts individually – how blockchain affects the supply chain, how decentralized finance (DeFi) impacts the banking industry, or how the metaverse changes customer relationships. But the real power comes from understanding the convergence between these technologies. In Chapter 2, we learned true exponential acceleration in business comes from the convergence of new technologies, that is, from the combination between them, and not necessarily from them individually or in an isolated context.

Nevertheless, our current education system is programmed to create experts in an isolated field. It all started around 12,000 years ago when people began working in the fields and farming. Hunter and gatherers, who traveled to the Fertile Crescent in the Middle East in search of food, began harvesting wild grains they found growing there and scattered spare grains on the ground to produce more food. Over the years, with the surplus of food some rural producers had, people were able to contribute to their community in other ways, which spawned the development of new professions such as doctors, artists, and carpenters. Rather than dedicating themselves to agriculture, they took care of other areas of society, solving problems that arose as populations grew.

With that came an educational model in which built paths shaped people from generalists, in terms of knowledge, into specialized professionals. This model is a reflection of what we have today, where our lives are lived in two stages. The first stage is where we learn the theory related to the field we want to work in, then we enter a new stage where we apply this knowledge in productive ways to earn a living and benefit society. The first stage is based on learning, and the second is focused on being compensated through work by applying what we've learned in that specialized field.

Around age 18, we are told we need to begin thinking about what we are going to do with our lives. Even though we study many different fields and learn many different subjects over the years, we are naturally guided by the education system to make decisions about our path to become more of an expert in a particular subject matter. As we apply to college, we are expected to choose a specialized educational path to take, which will then support our future careers. This mentality teaches us we need to have clear plans and ambitions for our lives, and then become experts in a certain field of knowledge, whether it's law, medicine, finance, engineering, or arts. Although I followed this pattern of upbringing, it never felt right to me. Why were we being forced to hyperspecialize in an overly complex and multifaceted world?

The convergence of Web3 technologies calls for a new understanding of the way we process knowledge, called cognitive flexibility. Cognitive flexibility is a term in psychology to explain the ability to jump between different areas, tasks, and mental groups. In its simplest form, it is the ability to quickly jump between various areas of knowledge. F. Scott Fitzgerald famously wrote, "The test of first-rate intelligence is the ability to hold two opposing ideas in mind at the same time and still retain the ability to function." Cognitive flexibility is exactly that. It allows us to navigate the complexity and multiplicity of Web3 technologies, digital identities, and areas of knowledge. It is a critical core skill of a meta-leader.

Today, we look at the Internet as a single, centralized, digital world, and we are educated to think in a specialized and linear way. All of this goes against any logic in the world of Web3. In Web3, there are infinite variables that affect our businesses, determined by the convergence of Web3 technologies, multiple identities, and even multiple metaverses.

The same is true in leadership. Traditionally, a leader's cognition is evaluated based on the depth of knowledge and the array of experiences they have in their field of work, mainly because businesses have been traditionally product-centric. Product-centric businesses place all of their focus on products and develop new and advanced products irrespective of their demand in the market. All the strategies and business processes are built around these products and work accordingly. While there are many advantages to this model, such as gaining an advantage over competitors and building the best product, it is also very limiting. As a consequence of product-centricity, leaders develop a very deep understanding and specific knowledge of their product, service, and market, which was successful in a world before technology where the customer was not nearly as empowered as they are today.

In the last few years though, technology convergence has empowered customers more and more as a result of three new elements:

1. Granting customers access to more information.

2. Lowering switching costs, which are the costs associated with switching suppliers.

3. Empowering customers to create content around their experiences, mainly through social media, which gives them a voice.

Thanks to the transparent and ubiquitous information available on the Internet, customers of any business can read reviews, compare prices, browse content, and learn about products and their sustainability. Information is power. Until recently, doctors were the only ones who had access to information about drugs and their effects. Nowadays, patients can inform themselves using Google before going for a medical visit, as long as they are aware of and able to filter out any false information.

Before digitalization, customers had fewer options, so they were often loyal to a particular business, even if they had bad service or were charged higher rates, simply because they didn't have any other options or the other option had additional expenses in terms of time and travel. In economic theory, these costs are called switching costs, which are the time, effort, and/or financial costs related to switching to another supplier. In the pre-digital world, they were high. Today, if a customer doesn't like the service or finds the fees too high, they can open an account with a competitor in just a few clicks, reducing the switching costs to practically zero. Infinite access to information and greater competition between companies have lowered switching costs, which has greatly empowered the customer.

Last but not least, with smartphones becoming an extension of our bodies and even our brains, customers can create content and talk about their experiences all the time. A bad experience can become a business's biggest nightmare because everyone will know about it. On the flip side, a good experience can make loyal and happy customers a marketing arm, as they share these good experiences with the rest of the customer base.

Imagine living in a world where each interaction you have with someone results in a rating from 0 to 5, like star ratings in Uber. You can give a rating to another person, and they can rate you in return. You have been served well by a waiter at your favorite restaurant, so you give him 5 stars. Because you tip him generously, he gives you 5 stars as well. After having had your lunch, you hop on the elevator heading to your office, and bump into a colleague. You don't like her, but you chit-chat and fake a smile. She sees that, and as soon as she steps out of the elevator, she gives you 3 stars, which ultimately lowers your rating. Everything is rated, from your every interaction to every post on social media. Most importantly, everyone can see your rating, as if it's tattooed on your face or displayed as a digital hologram on top of your head. This may seem familiar if you've watched the third season of Netflix's *Black Mirror* series. Under this level of massive scrutiny, would you act the same way you're acting today in the real world, or would you behave differently?

Most people would likely modify their behaviors to please others and get a higher rating. Have you ever rented out your home through Airbnb? I have, and I double-check the house twice before someone's stay to make sure everything is perfectly in place, all because I want those 5 stars. This isn't something I would do if renting the apartment out to my cousin's friend though. Based on my Superhost rating (yes, I can proudly boast a 4.98 rating), Airbnb's algorithm rewards me by promoting my listing in their searches.

Digitization increases the rate at which technology evolves exponentially, consequently putting pressure on these specialists throughout their lives in two ways. First, jobs change over the course of a single career, so people need to constantly update themselves. This is proven by recent statistics by Dell Technologies, which says 85% of jobs that will exist in 2030 have not been invented yet. Second, being an expert is not enough in a more complex and interconnected world, which is why meta-leaders need to practice cognitive flexibility as a way of bringing together different areas of knowledge to gain a competitive advantage.

Cognitive flexibility is the strongest skill of the professionals and leaders David Epstein calls "specialized generalists" in his book *Range: Why Generalists Triumph in a Specialized World.* Specialized generalists are those who can combine vertical and specialized thinking with lateral thinking. The term lateral thinking was first coined by Edward de Bono in 1967 as a direct contrast to forward thinking. Lateral thinking refers to any use of pre-existing knowledge in a new context. Specialists assume new, undiscovered knowledge and technology is the key to innovation, but Epstein argues this isn't necessarily the case.

Often, old ideas used in a new way are more valuable than cutting-edge discoveries, such as duct tape. The construction workers who popularized duct tape were simply repurposing an older tape they had used to seal ammunition boxes during World War II. Now, duct tape is a multi-purpose solution you can find in most households.

Our cognitive flexibility is more than just our ability to jump to quick conclusions based on our pre-existing knowledge. It is also being able to read our external environment for context and explore multiple fields of knowledge to solve new business problems because, as we know, contexts change all the time.

As a teenager, I used to work over the summer as a lifeguard in Celle Ligure, a beach near Genoa. To become a lifeguard, I was required to take a course and pass a final exam to receive my certification. Soon after my 16th birthday, I registered for the course and discovered it would take six months to complete. I was shocked. At the time, I thought it would only take a couple of weeks. The job seemed so easy – you just watch the sea – and the Mediterranean was so calm, it wasn't likely anything would ever happen. But after the first class, I understood why. The sea is never the same; it is always changing.

While the Mediterranean is usually relatively calm, the lifeguard course was preparing us for all possible scenarios an ever-changing sea can bring. You never know when you may need to rescue someone in rough waters, huge waves, or a strong current. The sea can be extremely cold or even induce electric shocks in the middle of a storm as the waters attract lightning. If you only train in a controlled environment like a pool, even if you repeat the rescue techniques more than 10,000 times, you will not be prepared for the infinite weather conditions and the unpredictability of the real-world sea.

In a rapidly changing world, we have to prepare for all scenarios and contexts in life and business. Heraclitus of Ephesus, a philosopher who lived in 500 BC, used the analogy of water to describe the inherent dynamism of the world. He said we will never step into the same river twice because the river changes all the time and new water constantly flows into it. Because of this, he came up with the Greek expression "panta rei," meaning everything flows, which assumes everything is always in movement and nothing remains static. This concept is not limited to the physical flow of rivers though; it applies to life and business as well and reinforces the idea that the only constant in life is change.

Although the majority of our education, training, and development are taught through repetition, that's not always the best approach. In Malcolm Gladwell's book *Outliers*, he examines the factors that have led individuals and companies to succeed and become outliers. He determines part of their success is attributed to what he calls the "10,000-Hour Rule," which states the key to achieving a level of complete mastery of any skill is to practice that skill for 10,000 hours. Doing a quick calculation, that would be 20 hours a week for ten years, 40 hours a week for five years, or 100 hours a week for two years. Since one week only has 168 hours, we have to be realistic and understand it is humanly impossible to dedicate close to 100 hours every week to just one activity, especially if you're someone who enjoys eating, sleeping, and spending time with family and friends. So, if you want to excel in a certain area, you need five to ten years of practice.

I don't disagree with this rule. If you practice any skill for an extended period of time, you're more than likely to master it. However, this theory doesn't apply in the current world of Web3 for one reason: when you spend so much time repeating a task or habit, you miss out on the opportunities to develop multiple other skills, abilities, or knowledge, creating an enormous opportunity cost. While the world today still requires specialists, it also requires our specialists to practice cognitive flexibility as meta-leaders.

Even though I followed the traditional path prescribed by our educational system, I remained flexible, which impacted my career trajectory. I am an Italian, who studied Latin, Ancient Greek, and philosophy in a humanities high school. After graduating high school, I moved to Milan to pursue my degree in economics. During my last year of college, when everyone else decided to do their exchange program in the US, I decided to do mine in Egypt, where I studied Arabic for six months at the American University in Cairo. Then, I went back to Italy, where my first internship was at Italmatch Chemicals, my father's chemical company. After that, I pursued my Master in International Relations at Johns Hopkins in DC, and during my second year, I worked as a consultant to the Department of State in a renewable energy project in El Salvador. From there, I moved to Brazil and worked with tech startups like Groupon and Tinder. Then, I worked at L'Oreal, where I pushed the digital transformation agenda. Now, I work as a keynote speaker.

For the longest time, when someone asked me the classic question, "So, what do you do?" I had no clue how to answer it. But when I began to understand more about the digital world, this frustration turned into an understanding that the secret of successful leaders and professionals lies in their ability to follow nonlinear paths, unlearn and relearn all the time, and develop the necessary flexibility to be ready for anything under constantly changing circumstances. These are exactly the skills needed in a world with multiple converging technologies and multiple identities for our customers and even our employees.

In the real world, our identity is our most important asset – it's literally who we are. Just as identity and authentication play such an important role in today's physical and digital worlds, Web3 will also require people to claim their identities. Yes, *identities* – not identity. Although you may think one person only has one identity, we all have multiple identities in the real world too. We likely dress differently at the office than we do at home. We behave differently around our family during the holidays than we do on a Friday night at the club with our friends. We may be quiet and shy offline but be outspoken, angry commentators online. Though this doesn't mean we are different people, it does mean we have multiple identities or different ways we present ourselves. In the metaverse and its infinite worlds, we will have exponentially more identities than in the physical world.

Overall, Web3 raises a lot of questions about the future of digital identities and online authenticity. Some of the most pressing are:

- How can individuals and businesses authentically represent themselves online?

- What does digital identity mean in this next iteration of the Internet, where the line between the physical and the digital is blurred?

- How can individuals and businesses manage their multiple identities in multiple metaverses that serve multiple purposes?

- How can people know who is hiding behind an avatar?

These fundamentally ask us to contemplate multiple identities in Web3. If we don't think about people's requirements, their identities, and the lifecycle of these new identities, we will create services that don't live up to the expectations of our users.

Navigating a world of multiple customer identities is very challenging and complex for leaders who are hyperspecialized. When we add in all the technology convergence, the degree of complexity multiplies. But, one way of looking at the world is to think of it as a learning environment in which you must develop new skills and abilities in accordance with the *zeitgeist*. These environments can change and range from welcoming to hostile.

Welcoming learning environments are environments where it is very clear what everyone has to do because the goals are outlined, the rules are clear, and the standards are defined. Tasks do not change much in welcoming environments. On the other hand, hostile learning environments are where information is asymmetrical and incomplete, there are no clear rules, tasks change all the time, and the feedback you receive is delayed and unclear.

In a pre-digital world, businesses underwent linear changes, so a leader's learning and evolution were made in a welcoming environment. However, the digital world creates a hostile learning environment as a result of constant and exponential change. Leaders of businesses today now have to have the cognitive flexibility to learn and evolve successfully. Through cognitive flexibility, leaders can take insights from one area of knowledge and apply them creatively to another.

If you could go back in time more than 2,000 years ago and witness a speech by Socrates, standing in the audience side by side with his disciple Plato, you would likely be fascinated to watch Socrates use his philosophical argument method called "maieutics." This method is based on asking questions to find any flaw in the discourse of an intellectual adversary. Socrates fundamentally used dialogue to discredit the claims of knowledge by others and ended up revealing the ignorance of his conversational partner. Through maieutics, Socrates' objective was to make us progress towards a more adequate understanding of topics, such as morals and ethics.

Today, most of us would see these debates as a huge waste of time because philosophy, in general, has always been seen as an abstract, intangible discipline, adding little value to the real world or business, often leaving its study or neglected by leaders. But imagine sitting in a Tesla meeting room side by side with Elon Musk and a bunch of engineers, addressing an ethical dilemma – what should Tesla's AI-powered autopilot software do if a pedestrian unexpectedly pops up in front of the car while cruising at high speed?

The first option would be to program the software to swerve away from the unexpected pedestrian, which could risk the lives of the passengers in the car. The second option is to program the software to slow down but continue on the path, which puts the life of the pedestrian at risk. How does one program software to make the most ethical decision in real-time, in a scenario where the combination of variables is infinite and where the software will not always have all the information necessary?

This decision is likely one of the hardest to make for anyone with a conscience, but this is the type of decision professionals in all industries have to make more often nowadays, whether they are engineers, software developers, doctors, or business leaders. These decisions often involve how to best use technology, considering the philosophical dilemmas it brings along. Yet professionals don't have the necessary time available for long and lengthy philosophical discussions about the moral and ethical consequences. In the example of Tesla, the engineers likely need to make this decision very quickly, in that one-hour meeting window, because Tesla production lines can't stop without losing money.

These are all very important issues leaders, entrepreneurs, and society as a whole have to address every day, regardless of the industry they work in, because technology today is embedded in every business, in every part of our lives, and leaves no area of society untouched by its ethical implications. These implications range from data privacy to AI trustworthiness, from fake news to sustainability, and even mental health issues arising from social media usage. All of these require a meta-leader who has the cognitive flexibility to embrace these fields in their repertoire of knowledge.

Though technological convergence has empowered the customer, forcing companies to move from product-centric to customer-centric models, Web 2.0 hasn't been able to solve all customer problems. There are still issues related to data privacy (how the customer controls what is done with their data), trust-related issues (how the customer trusts the company), and the experimentation of products limited to the physical world (a customer cannot *fully* experience the real value of a product or service through e-commerce). With Web3, companies can improve their customer experience and achieve even greater customer-centricity in the future. Here are some of the ways Web3 can improve the customer experience in any business:

- More trust, since transactions and relations take place in trustless environments powered by the blockchain.

- More privacy and data ownership, since blockchain allows customers to own and control their own data.

- Hyper-personalization, in exchange for sharing access to data with businesses.

- Low friction in any customer journey, especially through interoperability.

- Instant gratification, since customers will be able to get things when and exactly as they want them.

- Less transactional relations with companies, as there is more focus on the experience.

- More collaboration as companies and customers act as communities with aligned interests.

Since we already covered the concept of trust in detail, we can go in-depth into analyzing all the other factors.

In Web3, end users will regain complete ownership and control of their data and enjoy the security of encryption. This means they will be able to choose whether or not and when information about them can be shared with and/or used by advertisers, marketers, researchers, and so on. One way to do this is with simple and intuitive interfaces on dApps that allow users to understand what information they are sharing with companies. This has the potential to give them full control over personalization and even get paid for sharing their information. Users could earn micropayments for survey responses or get paid with tokens for consuming or sharing content.

In addition to more privacy and more control of data, end users can get hyper-personalization for sharing their protected data, and AI is key to providing these personalized experiences. By leveraging many variables that reveal how, when, and what customers buy, such as contextual data, behavior, demographics, expressed interests, customer reward programs, seasonal data, and even information about the local weather, machine learning can identify patterns and use them to make predictions about customers' needs. Hyper-personalization has a great impact on businesses of all sorts because personalizing the user experience positively impacts the business. Research performed by the IT company Accenture shows 91% of consumers say they are more likely to shop with brands that provide offers and recommendations that are relevant to them. At the same time, another study from Adobe revealed 66% of consumers say encountering non-personalized content would prevent them from making a purchase.

Next, there is the benefit of low friction. Imagine a B2B company buying raw materials around the world. They need to place many orders, across different countries, with different regulations, and different taxes. This can be very complicated at times, which creates a lot of friction. With online stores and e-commerce, this friction has already diminished. In the world of Web3, this will be resolved with the concept of interoperability. Although, interoperability isn't 100% developed yet.

Theoretically, if you buy a digital version of a Zara dress on Roblox (a gaming metaverse), you won't be able to use it in another metaverse like Horizon Worlds by Meta because these metaverses are not "open" yet. For now, each metaverse is separate from another, preventing consumers from moving digital goods from one virtual world to another. This is extremely inconvenient, but it's not something we often think about because it's always been that way. Web3 has the power to change that. All our information and belongings will be centralized to our personal identity, be it a crypto wallet or a self-sovereign identity (SSI), as tokens. What we own will be connected to our identity rather than to a platform, which will allow us to take everything with us as we hop from one app or ecosystem to another.

This also has the potential to have a huge impact on the interoperability between IoT devices in general and those in smart homes and smart cities, which will already know us and our preferences. Wouldn't it be nice to arrive at your favorite hotel and the background music is your favorite tune and have the air conditioning set to exactly the right temperature you like?

Interoperability removes all friction between one experience and another, which is one of the great benefits of Web3, and AI helps to make interoperability possible. We all know what it's like to call a customer service number and wait on hold for hours before ever having a chance to talk to a representative – that's a lot of friction to solve a problem. Alternatively, we can now solve it via Whatsapp through an AI-powered chatbot, where there is usually significantly less friction. The latter scenario is likely preferred by the customer, and although chatbots are not perfect yet either, the more they interact, the better they become, through machine learning.

AI reduces friction in user experiences as a result of a subfield of AI called natural language processing (NLP), which allows customers to ask for precisely what they require using their natural language. This minimizes the number of steps required to finish a task or make a purchase and reduces the potential for customer frustration, therefore reducing friction. If there's too much friction, a company may lose its most valuable customers.

Web3 also brings another benefit related to the relationships we have with companies, which become less transactional and feel more like communities. One great example is the band Kings of Leon, who released an album as an NFT. Their tokens included a limited number of unique-looking golden tickets, which unlocked special perks like a limited-edition vinyl record and front-row seats to future shows.

Most current loyalty systems, such as airline miles programs, benefit the company more than they do the customer. NFTs allow for more engagement with customers, who will then become part of the company's journey. If I have a company's NFT, the company and I will both have shared rather than opposing interests. In other words, if the company is doing well, the value of the NFT will go up, and I will do well too. As a customer, I will benefit when the brand performs better, so I have the incentive to advocate for the brand to be successful. This might sound similar to having stock in a company, and it is, but tokens also offer additional perks. Companies can determine the perks associated with their tokens, and those perks could be anything from exclusive access to something within the company to discounts or special events.

Let's say you own a winery and create a "wine club," where customers get an NFT and receive four bottles per month for an annual fee. Now, imagine your wine brand becoming super popular, and its NFT value doubling in the first six months. Your customers can then resell it and make a profit. This creates more incentive for customers to participate in the community and not just interact individually and transactionally with the company. This is amazing for customer retention and loyalty. Outside of NFTs, you can have DAOs where members can decide on the next grape combinations for your wine and make other unique decisions for the direction of the company. There are so many added benefits with Web3, and creativity has no limits with Web3 concepts and technologies.

Lastly, Web3 enhances the user experience. When combined with the metaverse, Web3 has the potential to enhance user experiences in ways that make them more fun, relevant, community-oriented, and immersive. Insurance companies are now allowing customers to experience the simulated impacts of certain events that could occur to them through VR, such as car accidents and fires (non-life insurance) or illnesses (life insurance). Then, they can provide their potential customers with the opportunity to fully recognize the risks they may have been previously unaware of.

Cognitive flexibility allows meta-leaders to better understand their customer by understanding how they shape their expectations based on the best experiences they have. It's no longer just about their experience with the leader's company, with their competitor, or in their market – it's the experience of all their daily interactions. Aside from our customers' interactions and purchases with us, regardless of the market we are in, our customers also have instant gratification through apps like Uber, GrubHub, and the like. They have hyper-personalization and low friction through their favorite e-commerce platforms. They get sustainability by knowing exactly where their coffee bean was produced as a result of transparency by their favorite coffee brand. They also have immersive experiences through telemedicine and similar technologies.

Customers now shape these expectations based on their best experiences. As leaders, if we cannot use cognitive flexibility to better understand the multiple facets of our customers and their expectations, as well as the convergence of new technologies and the impact they have on our customers, we will not be able to harness the potential to expand our knowledge base beyond our realm of specialization.

CHAPTER 6:

Antifragility

I have always admired scientists for their ability to meticulously experiment and fail an infinite number of times before discovering anything new. Mistakes and failures are simply part of the discovery process, and if scientists weren't willing to admit they were wrong at times, we wouldn't have many of the technologies and advancements we have today. In fact, there wouldn't have been any experiments to begin with.

I was lucky enough to grow up with a scientist at home. My mother is a cancer cell researcher at the University of Genoa in Italy. As a teenager, I remember how she would come home from work with a smile on her face and tell me what a great day she had at work. In those days, I got excited and imagined my mother winning a Nobel Prize. But as soon as I asked her what she discovered, she would look at me perplexed. She would say, "I didn't discover anything. Why are you even asking me?"

Frustrated, I replied, "How can you say you had a good day at work if you haven't discovered anything?"

She would answer with, "Because I managed to do a lot of experiments, and even though they all failed, I learned many new things."

As a scientist, my mother saw the benefits of making mistakes, yet so many times in business, mistakes are deemed bad. Leaders want to avoid making mistakes because they don't want to deal with the consequences or the possibility of being perceived as weak or incapable of doing the job. The main and most obvious consequence in business is the financial cost. There is also frustration, loss of customers, reputation problems, inefficiencies, and many more. But, I challenge you to think about the positive consequences.

As we know from scientists like my mother, learning is one outcome. Then, when one person learns from a mistake and shares their learnings with someone else, they open the door for collaboration, which is another positive consequence. This also allows us the ability to discard options we know are less likely to benefit us when we aren't sure which direction to go or how to solve a problem. Mistakes can also make us stronger because they make us more prepared for what's next. Once we understand we can learn from our mistakes, we can change our attitude toward them and start experimenting more. It's not just about learning from our mistakes; it's about using them to make us stronger.

A few years ago, I backpacked alone through Asia, visiting places like Thailand, Laos, Vietnam, and Cambodia. When I arrived at my first destination of Bangkok, I decided to brush off the 12 hours of jetlag with some jiu-jitsu training, a martial art of which I am a black belt. This has become a tradition for me every time I travel somewhere new. Conveniently, there was a gym near my hotel offering jiu-jitsu and Muay Thai, also called Thai boxing. I watched the local fighters from afar as they got ready for training, and I noticed they were rolling glass bottles up and down their shins with extreme pressure for several minutes. I didn't quite understand what it was about, so I asked the trainer. He explained that this causes microtrauma injuries to the bone and kills the shin nerves, resulting in a stronger bone and greater pain tolerance. This contradicted my belief that breaking something made it weaker, not stronger.

In 1889, philosopher Friedrich Nietzsche wrote, "That which does not kill me, makes me stronger," in his book *The Twilight of the Idols*. Today, his words have transformed into a famous quote used by motivational speakers and have spread across the internet as a meme to promote resilience. Yet, the ability to become stronger through crises and mistakes goes beyond resilience. It's about improving through volatility and chaos, becoming stronger through failures, and not just returning to our previous state of surviving. In 2012, economist and philosopher Nassim Nicolas Taleb created a term for this called "antifragile." He defines antifragility as a property of systems in which they increase in capability to thrive as a result of stressors, shocks, volatility, noise, mistakes, faults, attacks, or failures.

When we think of glass, we know it is fragile. If we drop it, it breaks, and there is nothing else we can do other than safely dispose of it. Broken glass can be dangerous, which is one of the reasons children drink out of plastic cups. Plastic is resilient. If it falls, it doesn't break, but it also doesn't improve to become more reinforced. Antifragile would be glass that becomes stronger after it falls, rather than breaking. Although it can be hard to think anything like that exists, we can think back to the Muay Thai boxers' shin bones. When you break a bone, it calcifies and becomes stronger. Building muscle works the same way. Working out creates microtrauma injuries in the muscles, which end up increasing muscle tissue. If our bodies can have antifragile properties, our minds can too.

Imagine a world where you can maximize the learnings from your mistakes while minimizing the heavy costs associated with experimentation. Much like the Muay Thai fighters learned that rolling bottles on their shins would build durability over time, Web3 technologies like blockchain and the metaverse can help us do the same in the digital world. While scientists have control of everything that happens in the lab and can monitor all the variables to fully learn from their mistakes, it isn't that easy in business because we don't have all the variables under control. Think back to the mango example at Walmart. Does Walmart know in real-time which fertilizer was used by the producer to grow the mango tree? Obviously not. This is data only producers, who are another stakeholder, can monitor. Not everything is under our control.

In Web3, everything is measured and shared in real-time. As businesses, all of our actions, experiments, and pilots provide us with feedback so we can learn from any mistake. When launching a new toy for kids in the metaverse that requires assembly, Internet of Things (IoT) devices will be able to measure the dilation of the customer's pupil when they see the box for the first time, the average time spent looking at the instructions, the percentage of customers who spend more than two minutes looking at the instructions, the percentage who put it back because they found the instructions too complex, and even the percentage of undecided people who stare at the instructions without knowing exactly what to do. If the company then compares these metrics with those of the control group, the previous toy, they will know in real-time which toy performs better. In the event the new toy didn't have the expected outcome at the beginning, it is quick and easy to act based on the learning. In the pre-digital world, we couldn't measure any of this, and our mistakes taught us little to nothing.

The fashion industry can also use Web3 opportunities to better experiment and understand their customer. Farfetch, an online luxury fashion retail platform, launched a functionality in 2021 allowing customers to preorder digital clothes from brands like Balenciaga, Off-White, or Dolce & Gabbana. The site collaborated with DRESSX, a virtual clothing designer, to achieve the most convincing rendering possible of these pieces, which are then manufactured in the physical world only according to preorders. This format is especially attractive to luxury brands because it lowers costs and increases the success of new launches.

Web3 technologies like the metaverse and digital twins allow us to minimize our costs as much as possible. It is obviously much cheaper to simulate luxury fashion designs in the metaverse, than to mass manufacture outfits, distribute them to local stores, wait for the sales data to arrive, analyze this data, and possibly discontinue the product if the design is not successful.

To be a successful meta-leader in Web3, leaders need to be open to using its technologies to focus on execution. Web3 allows us to create virtual copies of objects, equipment, and even real people, so we can minimize the cost of experiments and mistakes as much as possible. This applies to every sector from the pharmaceutical companies, that can minimize the costs of clinical trials for new drugs by using digital twins, to the automobile industry, which can experiment with new assembly line formats of cars, similar to how BMW does in partnership with Nvidia. Even mining companies can use simulations of extraction processes to prevent, intervene, and minimize the cost of mistakes, which can sometimes be astronomical.

The COVID-19 pandemic forced creatives such as artists, musicians, and speakers, like me, to find alternative ways to engage with their fans since they could no longer perform in person. Because the metaverse is a platform for low-cost experimentation and real-time feedback, DJ Marshmello teamed up with Fortnite, one of the most-played video games in the world, which is also considered a metaverse in and of itself, to perform an experiment. They decided to do a show and broadcast it in real-time within the metaverse of Fortnite, exclusive to Fortnite's audiences. There was no guarantee this would work because people spent their time in Fortnite playing games, not watching performances. Because the costs for this experiment were low in the metaverse, they decided it was worth the risk. Well, more than 10 million people attended DJ Marshmello's show that day, which was a larger audience than any of his physical shows, even leaving DJ Marshmello surprised by the turnout in a digital format.

Meta-leaders need to learn to embrace mistakes, but they have to know which types of mistakes are beneficial. There are three types of mistakes:

1. Avoidable mistakes: These are bad mistakes because they represent failures in well-known and routine processes. They usually occur due to distraction or lack of qualification. More often than not, their causes are easy to detect, and solutions for these types of errors can easily be determined through checklists or some other form of standardized process or procedure.

2. Unavoidable mistakes: These mistakes are out of our control. We can minimize their probability through maintenance, but we cannot reduce them to zero. A machine in a manufacturing plant breaking down is an unavoidable mistake. Because we can't avoid these altogether, we should focus on minimizing their chances of occurring, since these mistakes are also bad.

3. Smart mistakes: These mistakes can be considered beneficial because they indicate an attempt to do something innovative and usually provide essential learning for the growth of any business. Creating an innovative product and testing consumer reactions in new markets are initiatives that involve smart mistakes. These experiments must be carried out on a small scale to verify the results and the feedback obtained, which could mean cutting back on experimenting if they fail or scaling them if they are successful.

Smart mistakes are good mistakes, and these are the mistakes meta-leaders can focus on in Web3. There are two main characteristics of smart mistakes:

1. Informative results: For a mistake to be smart, it needs to give an informative result, either because it's designed to provide feedback or because you're willing to reflect upon the learnings. We usually see the same mistakes over and over again because we don't reflect upon them or learn from them through feedback. This, according to Albert Einstein, is the definition of insanity, which is "doing the same thing over and over and expecting different results."

2. Minimize cost and scope: Smart mistakes are relatively cheap. Digital technologies allow us to design simulations of reality at lower costs. Two examples of this are 3D printing and digital twins. If a business creates a prototype of a factory in the metaverse, they can run experiments without the risk of breaking anything. As a smart man once said, "A mistake is only smart if you survive it." It is as simple as that.

Andrea Iorio

Overpriced mistakes can destroy our businesses, so they certainly aren't smart.

With this new point of view on mistakes, we can transform the way we look at failure. In a traditional model, failure is simply not acceptable. There is a belief that good leaders, entrepreneurs, and employees never fail, with the leader's role being to prevent and minimize failure. With this mentality, people avoid experimentation and hide their failures out of fear and to protect themselves.

What we need is the exact opposite – a new framework in which mistakes begin to be accepted as a natural consequence of experimentation and innovation, and where good leaders, entrepreneurs, and collaborators learn from smart mistakes and share the lessons with others. In this model, the leader's role is to promote learning through mistakes and admit uncertainty is part of the experimentation process and the digital world at large.

This new approach to mistakes allows leaders to foster an antifragile culture within the company. In the business world, antifragility defines leaders and companies who become stronger the more they are exposed to stressful conditions. The more they fail, the more they learn. As if each time they make a mistake, it increases their motivation and improves their ability to become better. Antifragility is the evolution of resilience. While resilience is someone's ability to move on despite mistakes, antifragility is the ability to improve as a result of those mistakes. Without improvement, we remain the same.

The ability to fail and make mistakes isn't without risk. If you work out too hard by pushing yourself to lift weights that are too heavy, you risk damaging muscle tissue. If you don't make immediate adjustments, you could risk long-term damage. Antifragile leaders should focus on reacting and adjusting to small mistakes right away, as they happen, so they don't become too big in the future. Failing to improve from small mistakes can make big mistakes more serious, so the longer without crises, the worse the chaos will be when a crisis occurs.

Antifragile leaders can create an antifragile culture. In the world of Web3, an antifragile culture encourages constant experimentation and a continuous ability to learn from mistakes. The main technologies of Web3, like blockchain and the metaverse, allow companies and leaders to be more antifragile.

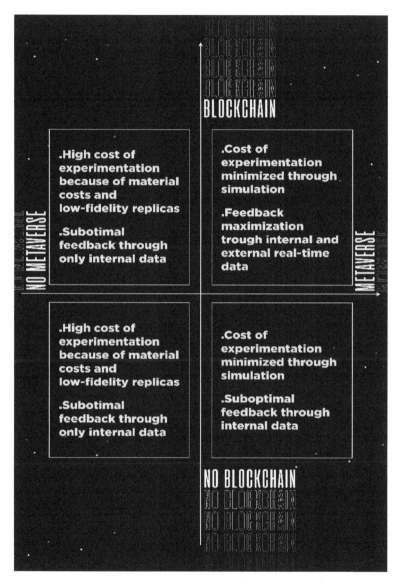

The Web3 Antifragility Matrix above shows the impact blockchain and the metaverse can have on experimentation costs and feedback. Blockchain allows us to maximize external feedback in real-time and transparently collect and access all this data. Blockchain's ability to collect data from a variety of stakeholders provides leaders with much better real-time visibility regarding the impact of their initiatives across their supply chain. As an example, TradeLens is a blockchain-based platform developed jointly by IBM and Maersk, supported by major players across the global shipping industry including shippers, freight forwarders, ports and terminals, ocean carriers, intermodal operators, government authorities, and customs brokers. Each entity shares information that can be tracked, stored, and monitored across the platform throughout a shipment's journey.

The TradeLens platform is accessible via an open application programming interface (API) and brings the ecosystem together through a set of open standards, also known as technology standards through which different systems can integrate. Powered by the Hyperledger Fabric blockchain technology and IBM Cloud, the platform enables the industry to share transportation documentation and collaborate securely, as well as provide real-time data to the stakeholders across the whole value chain - something unimaginable in the past. The result of this is much better decision-making and learning from experiments in real-time.

On the other hand, the metaverse enables us to replicate physical objects in immersive 3D environments, extremely reducing the cost of testing and experimenting, so we can scale projects and new launches after we've already proven them at minimal costs. In the business of designing planes, each component and part must be tested and certified for safety before the plane is ready for service, which can be very expensive. As a result, some in the industry have turned to digital twin technology over the last two decades as a way to potentially help lower costs, speed up testing cycles, and create model aircrafts before building and testing physical prototypes. To do this sort of in-depth virtual testing, many aerospace companies look to external organizations like the National Institute for Aviation Research (NIAR), the aerospace research and development branch of Wichita State University. According to a McKinsey estimate, digital twins can accelerate time to market by up to 50%, as companies can spend less time building and testing physical models. Digital twins are a game changer for the aerospace industry because they don't have to spend many millions of dollars building physical prototypes to develop and test new aircraft concepts.

Leaders can incorporate these two technologies into their business, obtaining extraordinary results when it comes to antifragility, especially when they combine the two together. If they resist these technologies, they will end up in the lower left quadrant of the Web3 Antifragility Matrix by not using blockchain or the metaverse. Then, they will end up with high costs of experimentation because of high material costs, as well as suboptimal feedback by only having access to internal data. In the event, they only incorporate blockchain but not the metaverse, they will have feedback maximization through internal and external real-time data at hand but still have a high cost of experimentation. On the flip side, if they incorporate the metaverse but not blockchain, they will have low costs of experimentation thanks to high-fidelity replicas but suboptimal feedback only based on internal data. The best-case scenario is to combine the use of blockchain and metaverse to maximize the internal and external real-time feedback and minimize the costs of experimentation through digital twins.

The combination of the two is extremely powerful. At the macro level, blockchain enables the storage of information in a decentralized manner with no single point of control. Fresh transactions can be added, but the existing ones cannot be changed or corrupted. This clearly ensures transparency and data integrity. Creating digital twins on a blockchain would mean all information regarding a physical product can be saved immutably. Taking it a step further, the product's transaction records can be saved. This means prospective buyers can get all the information about the product since its origin. This will create a proof of authenticity and identity. Keeping a digital twin, or more specifically a digital certificate, on blockchain helps businesses retain information about their products perpetually and securely. The data regarding transactions for these products also can be saved on a blockchain.

In the energy industry, digital twins and blockchain can be used in the utility sector to help utility operators efficiently fulfill their consumers' requirements. Because the production and consumption of energy vary greatly based on consumer behavior, electricity meters in our homes are now embedded with IoT sensors to become smart electricity meters. These connected meters can directly communicate the consumption data every few minutes to the smart energy grid. The energy consumption details of every individual consumer can be digitally updated on the blockchain to guarantee transparency. The corresponding digital twin for the smart energy grid can receive and analyze the energy consumption data to generate actionable insights through AI, giving energy service providers a clear understanding of the consumer's behavior.

Antifragility is not an easy feat for leaders though because we crave certainty and control. As leaders, we have a natural tendency to want to control all the variables in our businesses, especially the outcomes, which is why we avoid mistakes and fear them. We ask ourselves, "What will the impact of this project be on my business?" and "What will our customers' new expectations be?" These questions are natural consequences of the inherent uncertainty of the future in business and life. We ask ourselves these questions, sometimes obsessively, as a way of trying to correctly predict the future.

Humans, as a species, are emotionally addicted to certainty. Psychologist David Rock wrote, "Your brain craves certainty and avoids uncertainty like it's pain," in his article "Hunger for Certainty." For humans, the desire for certainty is inborn; it is part of the wiring of the brain. While certainty rewards the brain with a feeling of satisfaction, a sense of uncertainty about the future generates a strong threat response in our limbic system. The more ambiguity, the greater the threat, and the more the brain's amygdala lights up.

We have always wanted to believe we can control the future and predict how it will unfold with a high degree of certainty. We try to convince ourselves we have enough data, computational power, and even enough confidence in our ideas that we can control our future through our decisions because we know these decisions affect our lives, the lives of our teams, and the fate of our businesses. The bad news is, our illusion of control has never been more than that – an illusion. The fact that we believe the opposite is nothing more than hubris, a Greek word meaning arrogance, which further depicts how wrong we have been at believing technology would enable us to foresee the future.

Businesses love to try to predict the future all the time, or at the very least, once a year when they budget for the following year, but we are actually very bad at predicting the future. Of the 4,000 predictions made by various experts in *The Book of Predictions* published in 1981, the majority of predictions were incorrect. However, some were on the right track, such as the prediction of the "wrist telephone" 25 years before the iWatch, but those were outliers.

Oftentimes, the decisions we make as leaders may go against our intuition. Imagine driving a car on ice. The car begins to slide, and there is a threat of losing control. In this situation, most people react by stepping on the brake to regain control. However, there are an infinite number of variables related to this situation, such as the thickness of the ice, the pressure of the tire, and the balance of the car, which, to the disappointment of the driver, are humanly and technologically impossible to have knowledge of. Rather than pulling the brake, where you risk getting stuck or spinning out, you have to do the exact opposite.

Though it may seem counterintuitive, the proper response is to maintain speed and turn the wheel in the direction the ice is pulling you. First, you have to accept you are going to lose control. Once you lose control, you have to focus on what is happening at the moment while still looking at where you want to go. There is no time to consider how long it may now take you to get there or how the car will look once you arrive. This is the information we simply cannot have before unexpected circumstances occur. Maintaining speed and steering into the uncertainty requires flexibility and adjustments to any deviations from the expected trajectory.

This scenario may seem pretty grim, but it is actually what moves our businesses forward. As the leader of your business, you are the driver and the car is your business. The ice is simply the uncertain and unpredictable world we live in. When you are driving on ice, you have to constantly make decisions and change your perspective along the way based on the feedback you receive. At each iteration, we are making instantaneous and incremental microdecisions that impact our future.

Although it might sound like a paradox, when leaders embrace the inherent uncertainty of the world of Web3 and AI, we end up having more control over the future than if we constantly try to predict it. When we are not limiting our range of thoughts, decisions, and behaviors to a narrow set that reflects the vision of the future we have created for ourselves, we have infinite opportunities to move forward rather than stop. By constantly pivoting our businesses in response to external changes in technology, customer behaviors, and the world around us, we do not only wait for the future to unravel itself, but we create it.

CHAPTER 7:

Autonomous Management

Before Ray Kroc became the founder and first CEO of McDonald's, he was a traveling salesperson, selling milkshake machines. Salespeople were necessary then and even today because they serve as intermediaries to bridge trust since there is no way for the consumer to obtain trust directly from the milkshake machine company. Digital technologies didn't exist yet, so the salesperson was the party intended to establish trust. The milkshake machine company trusted the salesperson, and the customer did too. Because Web3's blockchain provides trust and eliminates the need for a third party, these digital technologies have an impact on the job market and the way leaders manage their teams and organizational structures.

In a podcast episode, Naval Ravikant, an Indian-American entrepreneur and the co-founder of AngelList, said he envisions a future where there will no longer be lasting and exclusive working relationships, but where companies will fundamentally hire in a 100% virtual and real-time way, by project or by a problem to be solved. Employees will be available on recruitment platforms, where applications will match the company's needs and the candidate's skills.

In other words, a data privacy expert could wake up in the morning and open her cell phone to find notifications from companies wanting to hire her for the day, week, or month, based on their specific challenges and projects. One company may just want her to review an important data-sharing agreement with a partner of theirs, another may want her to participate in an important strategic board meeting, and a third might want her to lead a project to rewrite the terms and conditions for their e-commerce platform. She sees the corresponding salary for each job, ultimately deciding to accept the second and decline the others. Then, she adds it to her list of tasks and responsibilities for the day. This is very similar to many of the freelancing platforms today, but imagine if this was the standard hiring format for all companies in all markets and sectors. Web3 technologies can empower job mobility by matchmaking employees and companies in a very deliberate way.

The job market is changing. According to the U.S. Bureau of Labor Statistics, over 47 million Americans voluntarily quit their jobs since 2021, the most unprecedented mass exit from the workforce in recent history. Though many might associate these numbers with the COVID-19 pandemic, a Harvard Business Review article titled, "The Great Resignation Didn't Start with the Pandemic" argues the average monthly rate of voluntary resignations increased steadily each year from 2009 to 2019. The authors attribute this to what they call the Five Rs:

- Retirement: resigning from a position and no longer entering the workforce.

- Relocation: resigning from a position to work in another location.

- Reconsideration: resigning from a position as a result of a decrease in engagement or misalignment between personal values and company values.

- Reshuffling: resigning from a position in favor of a higher-paying position to attain short-term goals.

- Reluctance: resigning from a position as a result of hesitation or an unwillingness to return to an in-person work environment.

Although it's not another R-word, I would add technology to that list because digital technologies are increasing the liquidity of the job market. There has been an increase in lower-level jobs and a decrease in those willing to apply for them, which is creating a powerful and potentially troubling gap, ultimately tipping the scales in favor of automation, robotics, and AI. A disinterested labor force, a proliferation of low-level jobs, and improvements in automation are creating a perfect storm for smart machines to substitute humans.

In the book *The Work of the Future: Building Better Jobs in an Age of Intelligent Machines*, the authors highlight two faces of technological change: task automation and new work creation. When people don't want to do the work that's being created, technology steps in. The jobs with the highest degree of manual and predictable work run the highest risk of being substituted by either robots or algorithms, which are becoming more complex. This brings us back to the fear of man versus machine. If AI algorithms think faster and smarter than humans and store more information than them, it appears they could easily substitute humans altogether.

Since the first machines were introduced on a large scale at the beginning of the 19th century during the first Industrial Revolution, the substitution of redundant workers has been common practice. One particular situation was the introduction of power looms in England during the first few decades of the 19th century when skilled weavers were suddenly put in competition with machines that could weave better and faster. Facing wage reduction or replacement by machines operated by cheaper, unskilled workers, desperate weavers (later known as Luddites) waged a campaign of destruction targeted at the newly introduced machines. The British government responded harshly by hanging seventeen Luddites and imprisoning many others before the movement was dispelled.

Decades after the Luddite revolt, the perspective of entirely automatic production, without any human intervention, started to be formulated. In 1835, Andrew Ure, an early business theorist, believed improved manufacturing would replace manual labor entirely. That perspective has not, however, materialized. As more tasks became automated, an even larger number of new tasks, made necessary by new technologies or entirely new economic sectors, were created that required human labor.

This is why the discussion of automation and employment should not only be centered on the number of jobs lost. Instead, it should also focus on the creation of new jobs and the changing nature of work as a result of the automatability of tasks. In Web3, the emphasis is on how machines and humans can work together so repetitive and dangerous tasks can be relegated to machines and automated systems. This augmented collaborative workforce is the wave of the future and has enormous implications for employment in the automation age. It will redefine the relations between workers, their crafts, and their working environments. On one hand, workers can focus on more aspects that require creativity, social skills, and emotional intelligence. On the other hand, this could have a dehumanizing effect if workers' activities are nullified by robots.

With all of these changes in the job market, there are millions of questions leaders are asking themselves, such as:

- How do I create long-term incentives for my team to make a deliverable that's good for the business and not just good for them?

- How can companies train their people long-term if they participate in such a liquid market, where one day they are with you and the next they are not?

- How do you manage to create real-time, transparent contracts that have the right incentives for both sides?

- How do you find a less bureaucratic and universal compensation model when companies and workers may be in different places?

- How do you manage people in this environment?

All of these questions are extremely valid, and they can all be answered using Web3 technologies. Blockchain governs the smart contracts, tokens govern the compensation, decentralized autonomous organizations (DAOs) are the organizational format through which the people are managed (or manage themselves, rather), and AI is the "workforce" that handles the jobs people can't do, don't want, or find too risky to perform. With these profound changes introduced into the job market and people management, the role of the leader in people management has shifted.

To better understand how it has changed, consider the main differences between the work of a film director and a theater director. While the film director intervenes and corrects actors on set, interrupting the scene, giving directions, and fixing whatever is wrong while it is happening, the theater director has a different approach. He prepares the actors and sets the stage, but at the time of performance, he takes a step back. His actors then have autonomy, as he surrenders his control to the unpredictability of their improvisation. After all, no one wants to see a theater performance where the director is constantly intervening and asking for scene changes.

Meta-leaders need to act similarly to theater directors by managing their teams through autonomy. While many leaders of today act more like movie directors, the world of AI and Web3 calls for theater directors. In a 2018 article titled "The Art of Balancing Autonomy and Control," a team at NYU Stern

School of Business analyzed hackathons, a competition where teams collaborate to create digital solutions to business challenges, in the United States and addressed the need for balance in autonomy and control to achieve organizational goals without compromising innovation. In the hackathon, the best management approach was to support the hackers by setting the stage, then taking a step back to watch the innovation process as it unfolds. The same is true for meta-leaders when it comes to people management.

Excessive control always backfires in business, even in a pre-digital world. In an interview, Reed Hastings, founder and CEO of Netflix and author of *The Rule is No Rules*, discussed the people management technique he used in his first company, Pure Software, which he sold. He recalls how in his company, he was obsessed with processes. With each mistake someone made, he introduced a process to mitigate that mistake. The more autonomy he took away, in favor of processes, the more he managed to minimize errors. For many leaders, this might seem like a reasonable solution to people management, but on the day he managed to finally reduce mistakes to zero, he discovered all of his innovators, creatives, and disruptors had left the company. Excessive control is the enemy of engaging and retaining the best employees because it demonstrates a lack of trust in them, which is the worst demotivator for high-performance and proactive teams.

When I worked for Groupon as the City Manager of Belo Horizonte in Brazil, I started my job lacking two of the main requirements for the position: commercial experience and leadership skills. I had only recently finished my master's in Internal Relations, and my only professional experience had been working as a consultant. After a few months of work and extensive KPI analysis, I discovered if our sales executives had X number of meetings a day, sent Y number of emails a day, and made Z number of calls daily, they would have the ability to meet their goal of five contracts per week. On paper, this made sense. I took these numbers, changed daily targets, and continually checked Salesforce for updates, accessing the sales executives' agendas. At first, I was amazed by how all those metrics started to increase, almost magically, but none of this was converting into sales contracts. I knew something wasn't right, and I grew suspicious. In an attempt to regain control of my KPIs, I began to call the bars or restaurants where the meetings were supposed to be happening to confirm my teams were there, almost as if I were spying on them.

One day, I discovered the deception. Overwhelmed by the need to show they were meeting the productivity goals I set for them, some sales executives began claiming they were having meetings that never really existed. I was furious and felt their behavior was in no way justifiable. I sat down with each of the guilty sales executives and called them out. Even today, I remember the conversation I had with one sales executive.

I told him, "You betrayed my trust."

He responded, "Andrea, it's the opposite. You have been betraying our trust for a long time now, by checking everything we are doing. By doing this, you implicitly tell us you don't trust us."

At that moment, I realized I was the one who broke the relationship of trust first. While implicit trust in business can be dangerous, a "trust but verify" approach would have served me better. By constantly micromanaging my team, checking their schedule every day, and believing my magic formula would drive us to hit a target, I was implicitly telling my team I didn't trust them. In this scenario, I learned the relationship between trust and micromanagement is inversely proportional, meaning the more command-and-control leadership is implemented, the less likely trust building is to occur. Needless to say, the environment I created at Groupon was unsustainable and negatively affected sales results. Once I understood my role, gave up control, and encouraged greater autonomy among my team, sales started to grow again.

Giving people autonomy may seem risky or even impossible, especially because command and control was a successful people management style for many years, on which many leadership models have been built. However, the success of command and control is based on the lack of three key elements: transparency, sharing of control, and decentralized incentive systems.

Web3 technologies have impacted the *zeitgeist*, or the spirit of the time, which has changed the way we view people management. Blockchain has the characteristics of being verifiable and trustless since anyone can verify all transactions and interactions, and trust is now distributed among the different parties by consensus. By minimizing the amount of trust required from a single agent in the system (in this case, the leader), the control exercised by a single agent can now be distributed among many agents, creating more autonomy and initiative within a leader's team. In addition, smart contracts, which are built on the blockchain, make it possible to create the right incentives for employees to work in alignment with the organization's goals. In the Web3 work environment, smart contracts align the incentives, not the leader's control.

Traditionally, the leader's role has been an intermediary between the people working in the organization and the shareholders, who expect business outcomes such as growth and profitability. Leaders and people managers make sure teams generate a certain workload to help the business attain its goals, while at the same time allocating rewards based on the attainment of such goals. In Web3, blockchain technology and smart contracts can substitute that role by increasing transparency, efficiency, and trust, ultimately removing the middlemen, namely the leader.

When you replace the traditional leader, there is a change in the type of management required in businesses. This type of management, which I call autonomous management, is the same type of management that works in DAOs and is one of the five leadership skills required of a meta-leader. DAOs can profoundly change the role of leaders and the way they work by solving the agency problem, which is a conflict in priorities between the owner of an asset and the person who was delegated control of the asset. The most relatable example of this in business is that of shareholders (owners of a business) and managers (those delegated control of the business). The shareholders depend on the managers to carry out suitable strategies to act in their best interests, which are for the company to grow and increase its profitability in the long term. But sometimes the managers and leaders have incentives tied to short-term results, so they could act in a way that is inconsistent with the shareholders' best interests.

When we analyze legacy companies, they traditionally have a top-down organizational structure, including many layers of management and processes, employment contracts that dictate the relationships between people and the organization, and salaries that act as incentives for performance. However, with DAOs, the governing law, which is dictated by smart contracts, regulates the behavior of all the participants. Once the smart contracts are deployed, they are independent of their creator and can be governed only by a predefined majority of network participants, and tokens act as an incentive for network validators. DAOs could provide a new win-win equalization for each participant in an innovative organization when it comes to their rules of operation.

Although you might be part of a DAO, you can work on many projects for the same DAO or even projects on other DAOs. As DAOs proliferate in the future, instead of having one employer and a 40-hour workweek, we might see ourselves contributing several hours a week to multiple DAOs. At the same time, DAOs will allow us to focus on work that makes sense to us, while rudimentary, algorithmic work becomes automated. This will free up collaborators to be the most creative and useful versions of themselves and allow them to spend more time on high-value activities that fulfill them and less time on monotonous, superficial tasks. While 85% of today's global workforce is disengaged at work, DAOs will give people more freedom to choose projects whose mission and vision truly resonate with them, jobs that align with their strengths, and value-aligned people to work with. This can also help mitigate work-life conflicts, excessive workloads, lack of autonomy, and office policies that create workplace stress.

In a recent paper titled "Are Decentralized Autonomous Organizations the Future of Corporate Governance?," Thilo Hullman, a student from Otto Von Bisheim University in Germany, argues companies that share the governance features of DAOs perform better in the market. He recommends corporate leaders of existing companies have at least two options for adopting DAO principles in practice: they could either try to shift the company towards more transparent, collaborative, and less political governance structures, becoming more DAO-like; or they could set up a new DAO that acts as an independent vehicle to facilitate venture capital activities. For instance, Pfizer Ventures has invested in VitaDAO, a DAO that funds early-stage medical longevity research, proposing to contribute $500,000 USD to VitaDAO and participate in the governance of VitaDAO using the $VITA tokens.

Andrea Iorio

After all, the underlying premise of Web3 revolves around the transfer of power back to communities and challenging hierarchical structures and traditional modes of management. This will require a significant degree of adaptation for leaders in the future, where command-and-control leadership and centralized decision-making will no longer work the way they used to. Refusing to adapt and actively rejecting these new organizational structures and work formats can undermine an organization's ability to retain talent because employees will likely leave for companies with more horizontal and autonomous leadership structures. But if you're worried that adopting an approach based on DAO, extreme autonomy, and trustless systems will render traditional leadership roles obsolete, don't panic. Even with the decentralization of Web3, the fundamental prerogatives of leaders such as decision-making, people management, strategy, knowledge, and innovation will not be completely replaced by technology.

As long as leaders understand their role is no longer that of a movie director, but of a theater director, they can modify their management style to allow for more autonomy. Just like a theater director, the focus of a meta-leader should be to pivot away from control and micromanagement and gravitate toward setting the stage for autonomy and people development by engaging and connecting with their teams and stakeholders.

CHAPTER 8:

Step-by-Step for a Web3 Transformation

So far, we have covered a variety of technological and theoretical concepts in this book, and you may be left wondering what to do next. With all of this new information, it's understandable to feel overwhelmed. Trust me, I get it. When I left Tinder to take over as the Chief Digital Officer of L'Oréal's Professional Products Division in Brazil, I felt lost. Though I had an understanding of businesses born during the digital age, I lacked the basic framework to start a digital transformation process in companies without a prior digital presence. As someone who has been in that situation, I can tell you the worst thing you can do for your business is close this book, put it on the shelf, and return to "business as usual."

To accelerate a digital transformation in the #1 beauty company in the world, I started my research and came across the book *Driving Digital Strategy* by Sunil Gupta, which totally changed my way of thinking about digital transformation processes in traditional companies. He presented a framework for transformations that divides digital transformations into four broad categories, or blocks:

1. Reimagine your business: Scope, ecosystem, and business model.
2. Reevaluate value chain: R&D, operations, and distribution.
3. Reconnect with customers: Journey, engage, and manage.
4. Reimagine organizations: Structure, capabilities, and learning.

I used this framework with substantial success at L'Oréal, as well as many other companies I've worked with on digital transformation projects. When I began thinking about a framework to drive Web3 transformation processes in traditional organizations, it provided a foundation for what I needed, but I had to make slight adjustments to the blocks to develop a framework to represent the step-by-step process to design and then execute a successful Web3 strategy as a meta-leader.

If a small bakery in a small town wants to grow its business digitally, a digital transformation may seem onerous. They already have a small presence on social media, but besides that, they don't really do or know much about digital transformation. But before they do anything, the owner of the bakery needs to ask themselves a few questions before they start this process. As a leader, the first question to likely come to mind is focused on finances – how much money do I have to invest in this? But it's more than that.

Here are some of the key questions leaders will need to ask themselves:

- What technologies do I need to adopt to digitally transform my business?

- Do I do everything myself or do I seek outside help?

- How do I measure success? What metrics do I have to monitor to define the success of my transformation?

- How do I monetize it? That is, how does my current business model change or how do I open new fronts and new business models that allow me to generate more value for my customers?

- What processes are required? How do I change or adjust my current processes or launch new processes to be successful in this new transformation?

These are the fundamental questions no matter what industry we are in. Whether it's media, pharmaceuticals, finance, legal, or real estate, these questions are universal. The only difference is the answers to each of those questions, since they depend on the specifications of the market and the *zeitgeist*. For a bakery without any digital presence, the answer to some of these questions may be to professionalize their Instagram by hiring a local marketing agency. A sneaker company that has already advanced and matured in their digital transformation process in Web 2.0 would ask themselves the same questions to advance to Web3, but the answers to them will involve Web3 and AI. The sneaker company may decide to monetize their customer base by dropping NFTs.

To help you take action on everything you have learned in this book, I have created the Web3 Transformation Framework, which is a step-by-step guide to help you undergo a Web3 transformation in your business. These are the steps:

1. Diagnose
2. Equip
3. Measure
4. Develop
5. Launch

The graphic below summarizes these steps, and we are now going to dig deeper into each step so you can take action in your business.

Diagnose

If you were a doctor, would you prescribe medication to a patient before examining them and making a diagnosis? I would hope not. Yet, we do this all the time in business by rushing to implement initiatives before really understanding what is needed or prioritizing the opportunities with the greatest impact.

In the diagnosis phase, we have to ask ourselves three questions:

- What opportunities have the greatest impact?
- What are the low-hanging fruits?
- Where can we learn the most from what we do?

Dr. Sebastian Wurst proposed a model in his article "Web3: New Business in New Web" that analyzes Web3 transformation opportunities for traditional businesses across 2 axes: one that defines what is going to be transformed (such as customer interactions, processes, or business models), and another that defines what is it going to be used or built (such as Web3 technology infrastructure, products, or platforms).

	Use Web3 infra (blockchain, Edge, etc)	Build Web3 products (NFT, digital twins, etc)	Use Web3 platforms (metaverse, data marketplaces, etc)
Transform Customer Interactions	Ex. Smart contracts for order fulfillment	Ex. NFTs for loyalty	
Transform Processes			Ex. buy data from marketplaces
New Business Models	Ex. Monetize unused computing recources	Ex. sale of NFTs	

The idea is for meta-leaders to map out the opportunities at the intersection of these axes. For instance, we can utilize smart contracts as a part of Web3 infrastructure to transform customer interactions through order fulfillment by taking away the need for a customer to continuously reorder the same product. Instead, a smart contract between two parties can state the cost of a manufactured product, the timeline for the product delivery (from factory to consumer), penalty and bonus clauses, the responsibilities of each party, payment terms, and conditions for settling invoices.

Although this might not seem much different from Amazon's automated reorder feature, Amazon doesn't have access to or control of your at-home inventory. If you sign up for a recurring order of pet food, they will send you the recurring order based on a specific time frame, regardless of whether your previous one has been consumed or not. But with Web3 technologies, companies will be able to access this information because it is on the blockchain, and the smart contracts are automatically triggered to drive automatic fulfillment when specific factors are met, such as when the stock of pet food is lower than a certain quantity. Another strategy would be allocating unused computing resources as validators on a blockchain, which is another part of Web3 infrastructure, to create a new business model. These computing resources can then be monetized as tokens, creating a new revenue stream for your business in Web3. Another option is the sale of NFTs as a Web3 product, which is different from using NFTs as loyalty.

Brands like Nike and Gucci have been successfully selling NFTs as a business model.

To help you take the first step in this process, I have provided a blank matrix on my website for you to complete. First, consider all the areas of opportunity for your business. It could be the ones listed above or any other you can think of. Then, choose the top three opportunities you feel would have the most impact on your business. These are the opportunities you deem the most important. Then, using the Web3 infrastructure, products, and platforms, identify how you can use Web3 technologies to transform each opportunity for your business and record them in the matrix. For example, if you are a luxury brand, you might want to sell NFTs; or if you are a manufacturer, you might benefit from having digital twins of your equipment.

	Use Web3 infra (blockchain, Edge, etc)	Build Web3 products (NFT, digital twins, etc)	Use Web3 platforms (metaverse, data marketplaces, etc)
Transform Customer Interactions			
Transform Processes			
New Business Models			

Equip

We covered many of the Web3 technologies in Chapter 2 of this book, and we now know what they are and what their purpose is in digital transformation. Though, when we look at how we can apply these technologies to our businesses, we still need to answer two questions:

1. Which tools and technologies are needed for my Web3 transformation to happen?
2. Am I capable of using these tools on my own or should I partner with other companies? If so, which ones?

Depending on the results of your diagnosis, you might need to focus on one technology more than another, which is fine. However, the end goal is to become comfortable using all Web3 technologies. Since there are multiple tools, technologies, and tech partners available, we are going to review each of the four pillars of Web3 to answer these questions.

Blockchain

When considering how to use blockchain in your business, you will need to know which type is best suited for your objective. There are four types of blockchains:

1. Public: These are available to everyone to participate in the blockchain process used to validate transactions and data. These are usually used in a network where high transparency is required, including applications for crypto, such as Bitcoin, and for data validation.

2. Private: These are closed networks where only a set of groups are allowed to validate transactions or data in a given blockchain network. These are used in a network where high privacy and security are required, including applications for supply chain and verification of goods, such as the Walmart example provided earlier in the book.

3. Hybrid: As a combination of private and public blockchains, some parts are restricted only to one set of users, while other parts are made accessible as a public blockchain. This type of blockchain often includes applications for medical records and real estate.

4. Federated/Consortium: This is the result of a creative approach to blockchain, where a group of preselected nodes or organizations control the consensus mechanism of the blockchain. In a federated or consortium blockchain, the network is not fully decentralized, but instead relies on a group of trusted validators to maintain the integrity of the blockchain. This includes applications in banking, supply chain, and research and development.

Once you pick the type of blockchain that is most appropriate for your business and business goal, you must understand which level of permission is granted to participants. There is a big difference between permissioned and permissionless blockchains. Permissioned blockchains are focused more on private entities and companies to manage their data and operations, whereas the permissionless blockchain is created for more and more people to join and add their value.

To understand which applies to your business, the first question to ask yourself is how many data sources you have. The data sources are where companies get their data from. If the answer is one, you would go with a standard database, where blockchain can be used but it's not always necessary. If the number of data sources is more than one, you need to ask yourself how the access control works in terms of the levels of permission. If it is restricted, you can use a private, permissioned blockchain. If it is open to all, there is one additional question remaining, and that is, who verifies the data? If a third party or a group of authorized validators verifies the data, you will need a public or hybrid permissioned blockchain. If it is open to all, you can use a permissionless, public ledger, like Bitcoin.

You can answer that using the decision tree in the following graphic.

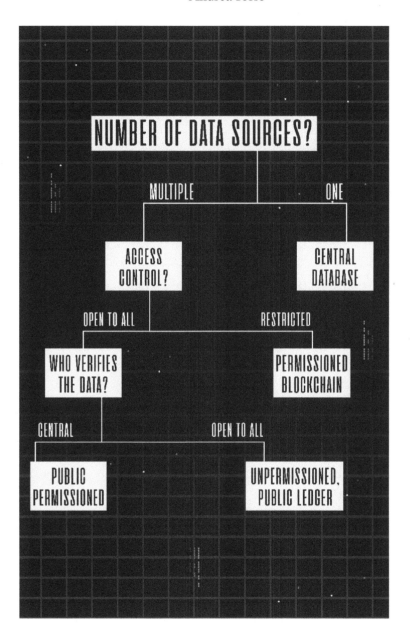

If you decide the best way to manage your supply chain is through a private blockchain, you then need to decide how you are going to implement it. You can do it on your own, build it on top of an existing platform, or hire a tech partner to implement it for you.

Building a blockchain on your own is extremely complex since you have to hire a team of expensive and rare specialists with experience in multithreading, cryptography, network protocols, and complex internal algorithms, as well as a solid understanding of modern operating systems to code the smart contracts, create the consensus mechanism, and reach the scale and network effects needed for the blockchain to work. This is a very hard and expensive choice for most traditional companies.

The second option is to work directly on existing blockchains, where you can decide to create your own dApps and implement custom consensus, transactions, and management of network validators. You can use ready-made, open-source code that has been tested on real networks, and you won't have to change the code of any blockchain nodes. In this case, you would still need a team of Web3 coders, and it still is not technologically very simple. Some of the most used Blockchain platforms are Ethereum, HyperLedger Fabric, R3 Corda, Ripple, and Quorum.

If this is still too complex for your company, you might want to consider the third option, which is the simplest in technical terms, to hire a blockchain-as-a-service provider. Many traditional companies do this already with cloud computing and AI. Some of the leading blockchain-as-a-service providers are IBM Blockchain, Microsoft Azure Blockchain, Amazon Managed Blockchain, and thirdweb (a provider born with Web3). Through them, you can join existing blockchains, build your own solutions, co-create with them, and partner with other companies. Technologically, it is much easier.

Thirdweb is a great example of a tech provider going beyond the traditional names such as IBM, Microsoft, and Amazon, as it is a Web3 native company that has built a developer toolkit — which currently covers more than 10 features spanning areas like smart contracts, decentralized logins, publishing tools and more — supporting a wider array of blockchains. In the early days of the Internet, developers also had to code websites and all of the features within them from scratch. Today, the same developers can build a website full of features without writing almost any line of code with tools like WordPress and its plugins. You can now easily integrate a payment gateway into your website with a few lines of code. Just like WordPress made it easier for non-technical users to create and manage their websites, thirdweb's platform makes it easier for users to build dApps, design smart contracts, and even create and ship an NFT collection in 30 minutes without writing a single line of code. Once meta-leaders identify the need to implement blockchain within the business, they need to understand which type of blockchain is best, then look for a reliable tech partner to minimize costs and technical hurdles.

Tokenization

Whenever we decide to tokenize an asset owned by our company, whether it is physical or digital, there is a step-by-step process to follow:

1. Select the exact asset to tokenize. It may be real estate, a regulated financial instrument, a physical commodity (such as a precious stone, artwork, or collectible), a piece of intellectual property, and so on.

2. Define the fitting token type (e.g. utility token, security token, NFT), which we laid out in Chapter 2.

3. Create a tokenomics model for the tokenized asset, which defines token supply-and-demand characteristics, outlines token value, and describes the rights associated with assets. Tokenomics is the study of parameters that determine the characteristics of cryptocurrencies or cryptographic tokens to create economic value.

4. Choose the right blockchain platform, which we discussed in the previous section.

5. Develop smart contracts to program the behavior of the tokenized asset, automate compliance checks with relevant legal regulations, develop blockchain-based asset management applications for token issuers and investors/token holders, and integrate the tokenized asset solution with the required systems, such as a crypto wallet, accounting software, payment gateways, verification services, and more.

6. Issue the token, usually in the form of Initial Token Offerings (ITO) on your own or third-party blockchain

platform to enable token distribution or primary purchasing of the tokenized asset by investors. You can also list tokens on user-defined token exchanges to enable tokenized asset trading on a secondary market, such as OpenSea.

This is not an easy or straightforward process, but when it comes to non-fungible tokens (NFTs), we have simpler processes such as basic NFT minting through platforms like OpenSea and Binance NFT, where you can smoothly turn your digital asset into a token stored on the blockchain. Once it becomes a digital asset, your NFT can be put into circulation and sold via smart contract. In the event you need to deploy smart contracts or customize them, you will need slightly more complex tools such as thirdweb and Manifold.

Initially, the NFT market boomed to the point that many players got into the market and generated a whole NFT ecosystem that provides solutions across the whole value chain, from aggregators like OpenSea and Rarible to tools for NFT financialization, secondary applications, and even infrastructure layers. There are many players you should consider when you look for partners to tokenize assets for your company. Although the NFT bubble has since imploded and there is much less hype around NFTs, there is a considerable trading volume of NFTs on OpenSea.

What is the asset you plan to tokenize?	
Which token type applies to this asset? (Circle one.)	Security, Currency, Utility, NFT
What tokenization model will you be using?	
Which blockchain type will you use? (Circle one.)	Private, Public, Hybrid, Consortium
What behavior needs to be programmed and triggered for the tokenized asset using a smart contract?	"If…then…" Example: "If the buyer's funds are submitted successfully, then the deed to the seller's house will be released to the buyer."
What date do you plan to launch the token for distribution?	

DAOs

Since DAOs work with smart contracts on the blockchain and have voting mechanisms, their development is not so straightforward. But as with blockchain and tokenization, there are tools that make setting up a DAO much easier than just directly coding the rules of governance on the blockchain. The first is Aragon, an Ethereum dApp that makes it really easy to launch a DAO with an Ethereum node and a MetaMask wallet. You can use their templates for setting up voting mechanisms. For instance, you can control settings such as support percentage (the percentage of tokens required to approve the voting), minimum approval percentage (the percentage of votes required to approve a proposal from the pool of tokens), and vote duration (the duration within which the participating members can vote).

After choosing the settings for voting, you can then set up the token by picking the name and symbol, entering the token holders or members of the DAO, and allocating tokens to them. Once you review all the information, you hit "launch your organization," and *voila*! It's much easier than coding directly on the blockchain.

There are other options as well such as Alchemy, which is a dApp built on top of DAOstack, a platform for decentralized governance of DAOs. Alchemy allows projects to seamlessly govern themselves, allocating shared resources and making effective decisions at scale. This makes it easy for DAO members to carry out three simple actions: create proposals for the DAO to take a specific action, predict whether a proposal will be approved or rejected by the organization, and eventually vote on whether a proposal should be accepted or rejected.

Another option is Syndicate, which is slightly different since it is a tool to turn any wallet into a web3-native investing DAO. It simplifies the DAO creation process, as much as legally possible, with the launch of its product called Web3 Investment Clubs, which allows users to create a group of up to 99 participants, pool their capital, and vote as a group on where to invest those funds.

There are a growing number of options to build DAOs more easily and smoothly. This innovative governance powered by technology is going to help more traditional businesses adopt DAOs and scale initiatives across research and development, supply chains, and cocreation with customers.

DAO Parameter	Description	Your DAO Parameter Input
Support Percentage	Percentage of tokens required to approve voting	
Minimum Approval Percentage	Percentage of votes required to approve a proposal from the pool of tokens	
Vote Duration	Duration within which the participating members can vote	

Metaverse

Besides blockchain, tokenization, and DAOs, one of the real challenges for meta-leaders is understanding how to best enter the world of the metaverse, or metaverses rather. There are many different metaverses, and they differentiate themselves based on a number of factors, including their degree of centralization and their degree of use of blockchain. We have metaverses that do not use blockchain and are also centralized, including games such as Minecraft, Roblox, and Fortnite. Then, there are centralized ones that use blockchain, such as Horizon Worlds by Meta. Lastly, there are decentralized ones that use blockchain, namely Sandbox and Decentraland. Knowing the differences in metaverses helps us know how and where to best enter when we want to engage with our customers through a metaverse. Below is an image to help guide you in knowing which metaverse might be ideal for your business to participate in.

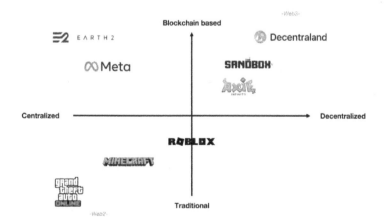

Another factor to consider when developing a metaverse strategy is the purpose of the metaverse we want to enter. There are multiple metaverses, many of which are related to gaming, but some are for socializing or working, and others are even perfect replicas of the physical world. Each one of them is populated by different target users, and before meta-leaders design a strategy for the metaverse, they should define the demographic profile they want to target. Once you enter the metaverse, in most cases by buying a piece of land and creating a brand activation for your customers, the sky's the limit in terms of what you can offer your audience, as we have seen when Nike activated Nikeland in the Roblox metaverse, reaching and engaging more than 21 million people.

But it's not easy to design and execute a metaverse strategy. In Nike's case, they acquired external knowledge about the metaverse through the purchase of RTFKT, a leading brand that leverages cutting-edge innovations to deliver next-generation collectibles merging culture and gaming. RTFKT was key to Nike developing the necessary skills to design collectibles for the metaverse and eventually sell them as NFTs. The results have been amazing, and Nike has generated the most revenue globally through NFTs so far.

Just like with tokenization and blockchain, there are tools to make it easier for traditional companies to enter the metaverse. An Estonian startup called Ready Player Me has built a popular platform for creating dynamic, animated avatars to use across the virtual worlds built and operated by others. The company today handles about 5 million avatars from across

3,000 partners. They are using their funding to double down on the idea that creating single avatars and identities that are interoperable (used across multiple virtual environments) will improve overall user experience and help grow user numbers.

Limiting your metaverse experience to a social metaverse, where you build relations externally with your customers, isn't a smart idea. A very important aspect of the metaverse is the virtual replication of any company's internal processes and equipment, especially for companies that work with complex supply chains or product manufacturing. This is called the industrial metaverse, composed of digital twins, IoT, and edge computing as technology enablers.

If we look specifically at digital twins, which are the main building block of the industrial metaverse, Nvidia's Omniverse is a great tool for designing digital twins. Nvidia is a scalable, multi-GPU, real-time reference development platform for 3D simulation and design collaboration based on Pixar's Universal Scene Description and Nvidia RTX™ technology. Today, it is the most used collaborative tool for the industrial metaverse and the creation of very realistic digital twins. Through Omniverse, Nvidia even launched a project aimed at tackling climate change called Earth 2®, a digital twin of Earth designed to simulate the effects of climate change in the future. Combining accelerated computing with physics-informed machine learning at scale on the largest supercomputing systems available today, Earth 2® will provide actionable weather and climate information on a regional level.

To design a metaverse strategy for your company, Jon Radoff proposed a framework he calls The Seven Layers of the Metaverse, which consists of seven tiers that describe the value chain of the metaverse market. These include opportunities, technological innovations, and solutions to our current problems.

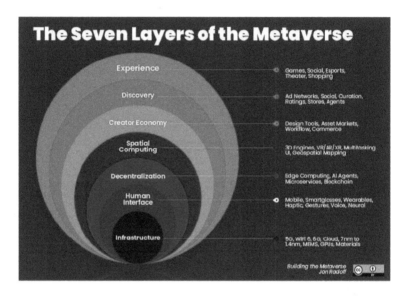

Infrastructure is the foundational base layer in this conceptual model. Without adequate infrastructure, none of the other developments are possible. Once you've developed the infrastructure, you can focus on the human interface. This is the key aspect of the hardware layer of the metaverse, which enables humans to interact within the metaverse. Then, you can plan for decentralization, which allows users to become sovereigns over their own data and products. Then, you need tech solutions that merge virtual and augmented reality and help us manipulate and enter into 3D spaces, which is where spatial computing comes into play. Since everyone will be able to become a creator on the web without having to spend hours learning to program, the number of creators will increase dramatically, so you will need to design your creator economy. Next, you will build your discovery, described as "the push and pull that introduces people to new experiences," mainly through content. Lastly, the metaverse will provide us with an abundance of experiences we cannot enjoy today, so you will create the unique experience you want your users to have.

Artificial Intelligence (AI)

Similarly to the other pillars of Web3, it is important to set up the right mix of partners and technology providers when it comes to AI. At the 2016 SXSW conference, Kevin Kelly, the co-founder of Wired Magazine, said AI is going to become a commodity you can easily purchase, such as water or electricity. He uses the metaphor of electricity to describe how AI will bring about a deep revolution in our lives. Imagine AI being generated in a faraway plant, and then sent to us over the wires, just like electricity. Just like the business of electrifying tools such as pumps, refrigerators, and other appliances brought about a deep revolution, AI is going to do the same. You won't have to create your own AI because you can simply purchase it, just like electricity.

Creating your own AI or even customizing existing algorithms can be extremely expensive and difficult. ChatGPT-3, an AI chat or developed by OpenAI, was extremely complex to train. It had 175 billion parameters that determine the end results of the algorithms, which required a lot of computational power, energy, and huge data sets for training. Because of the added expense to companies, it's better to rely on third-party AI providers like OpenAI rather than trying to create their own. Picking the right tech partner is essential when any traditional business is developing an AI strategy. Some of the major tech providers of AI solutions include: IBM through IBM Watson, Microsoft through Azure, Amazon through AWS, Google through Deepmind, OpenAI through ChatGPT, SenseTime, and Nvidia, especially when it comes to AI hardware.

Overall, artificial intelligence (AI) refers to the ability of machines to learn and make decisions based on data and analytics. When we think about AI being used by businesses, our minds likely jump to automation. But while some applications of AI do involve automating processes originally performed by humans, automation only scratches the surface of what AI and machine learning can do, especially when used by businesses. Most applications focus on driving growth. By embracing AI and machine learning, companies are finding innovative ways to improve business performance. Some business benefits of AI include:

- Boosting efficiency through process automation.
- Improving the speed or consistency of service.
- Improving the customer experience.
- Using customer insights to inform decision-making.
- Uncovering opportunities for new products and services.

Andrea Iorio

Think of chatbots. They are perhaps one of the most common AI technologies to interact directly with customers. From a business perspective, chatbots allow companies to streamline their customer service processes and free up employees' time for issues that require more personalized attention. Chatbots typically use a combination of natural language processing, machine learning, and AI to understand customer requests. We can also look at how streaming services recommend TV series or movies to their consumers by analyzing the types of movies and shows they most frequently click on. AI-powered streaming platform algorithms can also encourage you to stay on their app for longer periods of time by presenting you with similar titles.

Overall, the areas of impact and opportunities to use AI in your business are almost infinite, and they all relate to AI's ability to complement the meta-leader's human reasoning process with fast, efficient, and data-driven AI decision-making. With the rising popularity of Chat-GPT and many other AI tools, meta-leaders have no reason to feel threatened by this technology. Instead, they should embrace AI as a companion and an important component to making their work more efficient and more data-centric.

Measure

The third step in our Web3 transformation framework is to identify and measure KPIs to answer the following questions:

171

- What metrics define success?
- What are the new KPIs I should consider in the world of Web3?

Working with data and KPIs is more challenging in Web3 because of the overwhelming volume of new data points digital twins, IoT, and edge computing bring about. Meta-leaders will have to pick and monitor better KPIs with a high volume of new data points and data sources. To do that best, we have to identify the new KPIs for each new initiative in Web3.

For instance, if a company has a DAO managing a stablecoin such as a digital currency pegged to a stable reserve asset like the U.S. dollar or gold, they may want to start monitoring metrics like the unique number of token holders, the number of integrations (with crypto wallets, token exchanges, etc.), and the total value locked (TVL), which represents the sum of all assets deposited in decentralized finance (DeFi) protocols. If a brand is launching an NFT, it might want to measure the estimated market cap, the unique number of token holders, the volume traded, and its diamond hands balance, which is the number of owners who have not sold their first NFT collection.

Develop

For any new initiative in business to be successful, you need to develop a strategy and both internal and external processes to extract value – such as money – from it, as well as scale and grow. As a business leader, your job is to make more money for your business, so you're probably wondering how you can use these Web3 concepts and technologies to make more money. Several new business models are emerging as a result of Web3 including Initial Coin Offerings (ICOs), which are related to the launch of a native token of your company. This is a great way to monetize and secure investment dollars in Web3.

Another business model is through the sale of physical or digital assets that have been tokenized, especially when they have a high price (such as real estate) or are highly regulated and not super liquid (like some classes of financial assets). As we have seen previously, tokenization introduces liquidity and makes monetization easier. Part of this is also the sale of NFTs, which, as we have seen with Nike's case, is proving to be a very interesting business model. According to Dune Analytics, after Nike, the clothing brand Dolce & Gabbana is the #2 ranked company in terms of NFT revenues and has made around $25 million from the sale of its NFTs. Other major fashion brands like Tiffany, Gucci, and Adidas each made between $11 to $13 million from their NFT sales by the end of 2022.

Then, direct-to-consumer (D2C) business models are going to be adopted by more and more companies in the coming years. Since blockchain takes away the need for a middleman, there is a possibility of selling products directly from the producer to the consumer, which is already taking place through e-commerce platforms and will continue to grow in Web3 as a result of the decentralized nature of blockchain.

Last but not least, the community business model rewards members of its community to use more of its service and generates loyalty through NFTs. This is represented by play-to-earn models, which are often used in gaming to reward users with cryptocurrencies or NFTs for engaging in blockchain-based games. For example, you may earn an NFT by reaching a specific level or spending a particular amount of time playing each day.

Launch

So, where do you start? This is often called the "cold start problem," and every company faces some version of it. How do you get started from nothing? How do you acquire customers? How do you create value for your customers?

Once the business model is defined, it is time to design the go-to-market strategies needed to launch our new Web3 products and services to the market and the end users. Go-to-market is a plan to establish how an organization is going to engage with its customers and scale networks of customers. This is an area where we have already seen great differences between Web 2.0 and Web3. While many businesses today have to spend a lot of money on marketing and user acquisition to scale their products and services, Web3 will allow businesses to create incentives for their users to grow the user base and further establish network effects. Network effects are a fundamental pillar of Web3's go-to-market strategies, and they are based on the concept that increased numbers of people or participants improve the value of a good or service.

Back in the first days of the Internet, Robert Metcalfe, founder of Ethernet, gave his name to Metcalfe's Law, which states the value of the network is proportional to the square of the number of entities taking part in the network. These entities could be computers or even humans. The value is squared simply because it is the number of connections that can be formed. These network effects are key to Web3 adoption and success as they apply to blockchain nodes, metaverse users, edge computing devices, and so on.

Two of the most common go-to-market strategies in Web3 are airdrops and developer grants, both of which are based on network effects. Airdropping, not to be confused with the iPhone transfer technology, is when a project distributes tokens to users to reward behavior it wants to encourage. They can be distributed to all users on a given blockchain network or targeted to specific key players, and sometimes they are launched to solve a problem or start a project — to initiate early adoption or to reward or incentivize early adopters. Then, there are developer grants, which are grants made from a DAO treasury to individuals or teams contributing in some way to improving the protocol. This can serve as an effective go-to-market strategy for DAOs specifically, as developer activity is an integral part of a protocol's success.

Finally, once everything is in place, we can move to the launch step. Launching any initiative in Web3 should be done through a proof of concept (POC). A POC is similar to a prototype run internally to gain insights into the workings of a certain project. In Web3, this can be done without having to invest time or money, and it can be used as an efficient launching pad to enter the market. Proof of concept development for a blockchain project allows a company to pilot the blockchain solution before it becomes widely available, which, in turn, allows them to find out what type of problems the project may run into in the future. Using a POC is a great place to start when looking for ways of adapting to the times before moving on with any Web3 solution customization or development from scratch.

Once you finish the POC stage, you'll better understand your project's constraints and challenges. If your concept proves viable, you can move on to the prototype or minimum viable product (MVP) development phase. But if not it's not workable, don't worry – you can still adjust your idea or pivot without significant risk to your business, then launch again.

Conclusion

"The sad news is, giving information to people is just not a good recipe to change behavior."

- Dan Ariely

You can have all the knowledge in the world, but unless you put it into action, that knowledge is meaningless. Although this may seem pessimistic and frustrating, it's true. Knowing about the potential impact and areas of application of AI and Web3 on our traditional business does not imply we will be able to translate them into action. But that doesn't mean reading this was a waste of your time. In fact, the content of this book is critical to developing a new style of leadership to take advantage of the opportunities AI and Web3 bring forward to our businesses.

While many authors seek to answer all of your questions in their books, my approach is to leave you with more questions than answers, to generate the momentum necessary to begin a path of cognitive, behavioral, and emotional transformation. This is a journey of developing and improving the skills necessary to become better meta-leaders in a future that is already here and constantly evolving. But we can only succeed if we understand the mechanisms leading to a behavioral change in ourselves, our teams, and our employees.

The best way to explain how behavioral change works is through the analogy of a child's development. From the time we are born, our bodies undergo several transformations and acquire a series of skills, especially in the first years of our lives. Anyone who has seen the development of an infant understands how quickly and unexpectedly humans can learn new skills, whether it's crawling, walking, or even holding their own bottle. Parents and caretakers are responsible for stimulating a child's development through two fundamental factors:

1. Creating situations with as little friction as possible, so the child can develop the muscles and motor functions necessary for the skill.

2. Creating the incentive and stimulus in the baby, so they have the will or the necessary fuel to continue implementing the skill.

As part of child development, pediatricians recommend tummy time, which involves placing the infant on their stomach. Because this position is uncomfortable, it causes the child to activate the muscles in their back, abdomen, legs, and arms to try turning over. This daily exercise takes an infant out of their comfort zone and forces them to develop their muscles, balance, and other motor functions. Just like children, adults also dislike stepping out of their comfort zone and often give up

178

at the slightest sign of obstacles, which is why we need minimal friction to change our behaviors.

Think about the number of newsletters or junk mail you get in your inbox every day. Because the unsubscribe process has friction – even if it only involves a couple of clicks – it's easier to just simply ignore them, mark them as read or swipe right to delete them, than it is to follow the steps necessary to stop receiving them. We create all of our habits, routines, and processes in our lives and at work to save energy because a lack of energy is an added source of friction. Yet all of these habits, routines, and processes end up becoming our own worst enemies because they require a massive amount of effort to get rid of.

But removing friction is just the first step in the process. Once we create situations for a child to develop their skills, we then need to create an incentive that allows the child to identify the value in implementing these skills. In the case of tummy time, we want the child to understand the value of moving around on their own. We might incentivize them by placing toys just out of reach of the child, that way they will want to reach for them or use their muscles to move closer to them. Reinforcing the impetus of movement through positive stimuli is key to learning processes and behavioral changes in child development, and the same is true when it comes to our personal and professional development as adults. We can promote the development of our meta-leadership skills by creating incentives so the natural development of the desired skills takes place.

In the end, leadership skills cannot be taught any more than we can teach a baby to have muscles. They can, however, be stimulated and developed through a learning structure that involves self-knowledge, practical experiences, human bonds, and a conducive environment for the desired behaviors to multiply organically. After all, human beings are inherently social and relational creatures. While humans and animals share more similarities than we want to admit, our ability to cooperate with one another on a collective level is one of the main factors that made us the dominant species on Earth, according to Yuval Harari in his TED Talk "What Explains the Rise of Humans?" Our ability to work collaboratively, create innovative solutions, adapt to the environment, communicate, and practice empathy are just a few characteristics that set us apart. They have been encoded in our DNA and make us who we are.

What we have to reflect upon is whether our human soft skills can be measured and developed in exactly the same way as our technical hard skills, or whether we need a different approach. Though I do believe meta-leadership skills can be developed, we need to leave behind the dichotomy of soft skills versus hard skills, let go of the format in which the latter is measured and trained, and turn our eyes to more organic ways of developing them. We need to abandon the idea that teams of professionals are like machines made up of gears, with specific functions and limited ability to act. In other words, we need to

Andrea Iorio

accept human complexity, stop thinking of people as pieces in a production line, and alter our view of linear learning paths.

Oftentimes, those nonlinear paths are the best way to develop the necessary meta-leadership skills in the current world. The path I chose to undertake is the exact opposite of what would traditionally be deemed as expected from a business person. If you've ever asked yourself, "How much time and money have I wasted doing things that aren't adding to my professional career today?" I know exactly how you feel. Because my nonlinear path was inconsistent with the norm, I repeatedly asked myself that question, looking for the guiding thread in all of it.

It wasn't until I began learning about the unique characteristics of the digital world that I understood there was no guiding thread. Instead, I learned this type of nonlinear, diversified, and unconventional path allows humans to respond to a more complex, more exponential, and certainly nonlinear world. It enables us to develop the necessary skill set in the face of new technological developments precisely because it takes us out of our comfort zone and creates the incentive to incorporate and develop new behaviors, just like in child development.

Though experiences, formal learning, and even beliefs are fundamental, we cannot let them define or limit us. They are not fixed. Instead, they are the starting point for us to constantly practice reperception and recognize when our internal rate of change is disproportional to the rate of change in the external world.

Meta-Leadership

As a meta-leader, you need to always ask yourself, "Am I changing as fast as the world is changing, as fast as my customer expectations are changing, and as fast as technology is evolving in this third iteration of the Internet?"

If the answer is no, you are inevitably falling behind. We need both urgency and clear actions. It's no use having a clear notion of the need to change our skillset if we eventually fall prey to the same actions and behaviors we undertake every day. After all, the set of actions we take as leaders and in our teams ultimately define our company culture. If we don't change our actions, we don't change our culture. If we don't change our culture, we eventually don't change our business. You cannot transform your business in the world of Web3 and AI by dropping buzzwords at the yearly company convention, sharing information and content with your teams about the topics, or hanging up cool posters on meeting room walls. If all this is not accompanied by a behavioral change, your culture is not going to be transformed – and neither is your business.

Ben Horowitz defines company culture in his book *What You Do Is Who You Are* by saying, "Your culture is how your company makes decisions when you're not there. It's how they behave when no one is looking." If you close out an important meeting by loudly stating innovation is now a key pillar of your company culture, but at the next meeting, you refuse to move forward with an innovation project because there is a risk of cannibalizing a small part of your traditional sales channel, you do not have a real culture of innovation. The same applies to us as leaders. The sum of our reactions to life's events is what defines us as individuals.

So, as you flip through the last pages of this book and your head is spinning with questions, don't run away from your responsibility as a leader, claiming not to have control of this unpredictable and complex world. I assure you, you have the power to control the way in which you react to the sudden and uncontrollable changes of the digital world. In this new world, technology asks us, screaming at the top of its lungs, to develop a new leadership skill set in response to the new *zeitgeist* that AI and Web3 technologies and concepts are demanding. This new skill set asks for reperception, data sensemaking, cognitive flexibility, antifragility, and autonomous management in leaders of all businesses, regardless of industry, sector, shape, or size.

I'm excited to watch as traditional leaders transform into meta-leaders and these new meta-leaders begin rising through the ranks of business – challenging the conventional paths in an unconventional era of digital transformation. You have everything you need to become that meta-leader. It all depends on how willing you are to take the necessary steps toward your leadership transformation and implement these skills in your personal and professional life.

About the Author

Andrea Iorio is a highly-requested keynote speaker for digital transformation, leadership, customer-centricity, and Web3 globally, and has spoken to most Fortune 500 companies, in Brazil and globally. He is passionate about sharing his on-the-ground experiences with digital transformations for companies around the world, including Tinder and L'Oréal. Though he wasn't an expert on digital transformation when he began his first role as Head of Tinder across Latin America, his educational background in economics and international relations, as well as his natural curiosity for innovation and learning, made him a leading expert in the field as he shares unique concepts at the intersection of business, technology, philosophy, and neuroscience.

Andrea is an economist with a degree from Bocconi University in Italy, and a MA in International Relations from Johns Hopkins University in Washington, D.C. He holds more than 10 years of experience in multinational and tech companies, starting out as the Head of Tinder across Latin America and the Chief Digital Officer at L'Oréal in Brazil, and he is now an MBA professor at Fundação Dom Cabral in Brazil.

Andrea Iorio

He is also the author of 3 books in Portuguese including *6 Competências para Surfar na Transformação Digital*, which was a #1 best-seller on Amazon in People Management and Leadership in Brazil, *O futuro não é mais como antigamente*, and *Metanoia Lab*.

Ingram Content Group UK Ltd.
Milton Keynes UK
UKHW050009210723
425506UK00002B/18